easy to follow step-by-step instructions

Creating Pattern Brushes in Adobe Illustrator

susan rutledge

WILLOW BEND PRESS

Published by Willow Bend Press, Prosper, TX
willowbendpress.com

Paperback ISBN-13: 978-1-950019-16-8
eBook ISBN-13: 978-1-950019-17-5

First Printing September 2020
Cover, Interior Design and Illustrations by Susan Rutledge
www.susanrutledge.com

Library of Congress Control Number: 2020909413

Publisher's Cataloging-in-Publication Data

Names: Rutledge, Susan, author.
Title: Creating pattern brushes in Adobe Illustrator : easy to follow step-by-step instructions / Susan Rutledge.
Description: Prosper, TX: Willow Bend Press, 2020.
Identifiers: ISBN: 978-1-950019-16-8 (pbk.) | 978-1-950019-17-5 (ebook)
Subjects: LCSH Adobe illustrator (Computer file) | Desktop publishing. | Computer graphics. | BISAC DESIGN / Graphic Arts / General | DESIGN / Graphic Arts / Illustration
Classification: LCC T385 .R898 2020 | DDC 006.6/869--dc23

Photo by Nicholas Ray

About the Author

Seven years ago, Susan Rutledge committed to design a camera-ready brochure for a non-profit organization her daughter worked for. The simple project ballooned into a 20-page magazine, which was considerably outside her area of expertise. On the advice of a colleague, she purchased Adobe InDesign®, Adobe Illustrator® and Adobe Photoshop® and utilized on-line training to become proficient in using them. After the project was successfully completed, she continued to research and experiment with the software, developing skills that allowed her to publish books in several genres. The Pattern Brush became her favorite tool, one she devoted the most time to learning and the one she now shares about in this book.

Susan Rutledge, a graduate of Oklahoma State University, grew up in Ponca City, Oklahoma. She credits Mrs. LaVelle Wittmer, her high school Creative Writing teacher, with inspiring and encouraging her talents as a storyteller and writer. She published her first book, Barely a Bunny in 2004 and has since published three more children's books, multiple journals and two gift books. She and husband Grant reside in Prosper, Texas. They have four married children and eleven grandchildren.

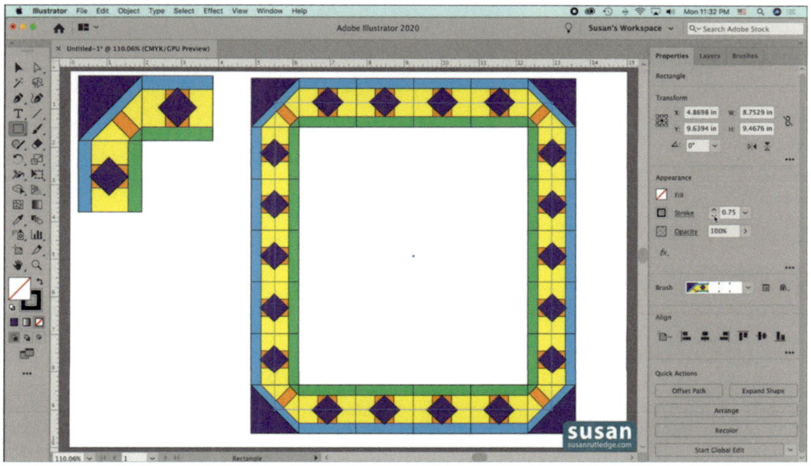

Don't Miss These!

Creating Pattern Brushes in Adobe Illustrator

Step-By-Step Online Training Videos

by Susan Rutledge

Table of Contents

Preface 7

Intro to Pattern Brushes....9

What's a Pattern Brush?....10

How Does It Work?....11

Tips and Time Savers....12

When an Object Can't Be a Pattern Brush....13

Creating Side Tiles....15

Creating a Pattern Brush....16

Single Object Side Tiles....17

Multiple Object Side Tiles....18

Text Side Tiles....19

Overlapping Seamless Side Tiles....20

Interlocking Seamless Side Tiles....21

Seamless Side Tiles with Color Stroke....22

Creating Doodle Art Side Tiles....23

Creating Corner Tiles....25

Auto Generated Corner Tiles....26

Making an Outer Corner Tile....27

Making an Inner Corner Tile....28

Editing Auto Generated Corner Tiles....29

Adding Corner Tiles to the Brushes Panel....30

Use the Swatches Panel When Simple Doesn't Work....30

Think Outside the Box....31

Creating Start and End Tiles....33

Start and End Tiles With the Same Height....34

Start and End Tiles With Different Heights....35

More Start and End Tiles....36

Challenges With Directional End Tiles....37

Colorization of Pattern Brushes....37

Spacing, Fitting and Flipping 39
- Resizing a Pattern Brush 40
- Fit Options 41
- Spacing Options For Pattern Brushes 42
- Negative Spacing For Pattern Brushes 43
- Flip Across and Flip Along 44
- Editing Shortcut 45

Ways to Use Pattern Brushes 47

Saving Pattern Brushes and Troubleshooting 57
- Saving Brushes 58
- Sample Pattern Brush Document 59
- What To Do If... 60

Preface

A Pattern Brush can be super simple or wildly elaborate. Regardless of its level of complexity, a Pattern Brush appears magical when it is applied to a path. The following pages delve into the nitty-gritty details of how to piece everything together, but it all boils down to one basic formula:

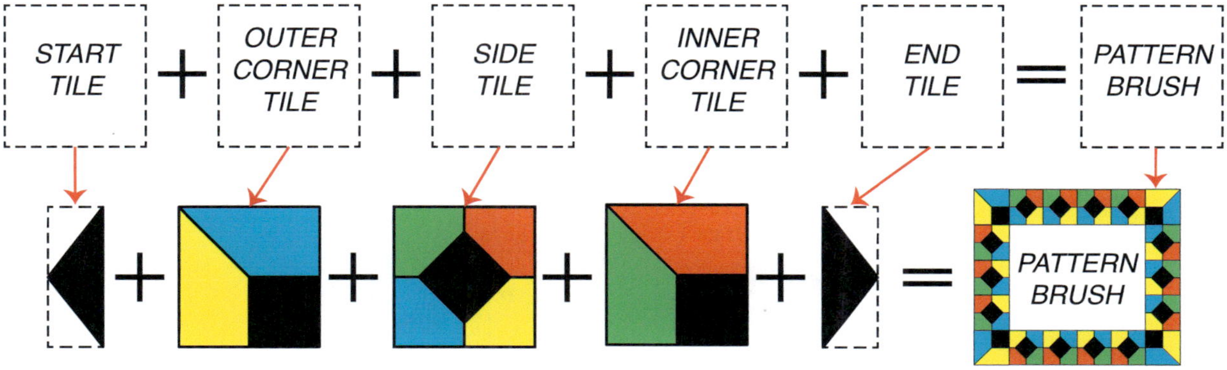

The tiles hold various parts of a design and flow together seamlessly to become a Pattern Brush. So what does a Pattern Brush do? It paints a perfectly fitted design onto ANY straight or curved path it is applied to. The range of uses for Pattern Brushes is as wide as one's imagination and can encompass both traditional and abstract applications. They are fun to make, enjoyable to use, and extremely habit-forming to play with!

Pattern Brush Tiles

(used in Pattern Brushes on the following page)

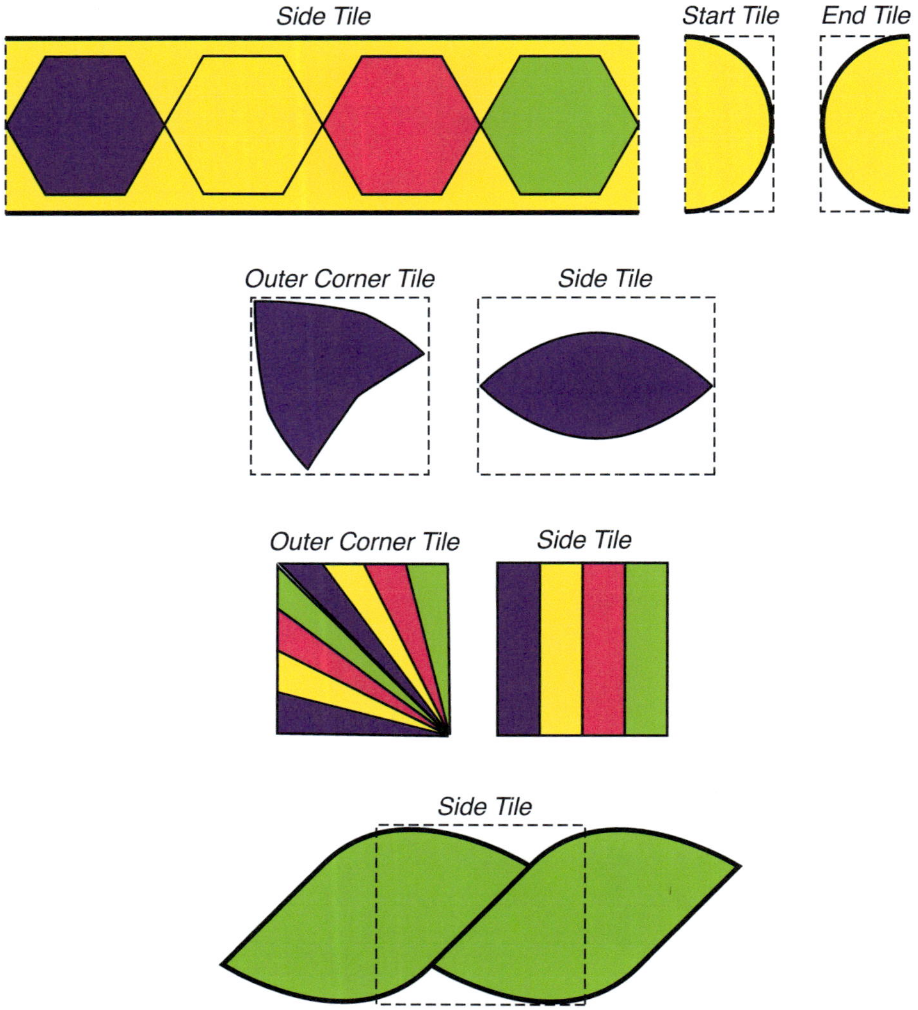

Intro to Pattern Brushes

Learn what the Pattern Brush tool is and how it works.

What's a Pattern Brush?

A Pattern Brush combines up to five different "tiles" to create a repeating pattern that can be applied to straight, curved, open or closed paths in Adobe® Illustrator®. The tiles can be simple or they can be multi-faceted, giving the appearance of being elaborate and intricate. Once the tiles are designed, a path can instantly be transformed into something beautiful with the click of a mouse. Pattern Brushes can be edited in multiple ways and reused over and over again.

Becoming proficient with a new tool requires training and exercise. Designing Pattern Brushes is no exception. The old adage is true...*practice makes perfect*. Have fun!

Samples of Pattern Brushes applied to open and closed paths

How Does It Work?

Each of Illustrator's Pattern Brush tiles have a distinct name and purpose. The main tile is called the Side Tile. It is the part of the design that repeats. Corner Tiles are used when a path changes direction. Start and End Tiles are placed on the two ends of an open path. Pattern Brush tiles are encased in an invisible rectangle called a Bounding Box. **For illustration purposes only, the Bounding Boxes in this book are displayed with a dashed line.**

The Bounding Box dictates how Pattern Brush tiles interact with each other and where they belong on a path. The Bounding Box will always be centered horizontally on the path it's applied to. Designs that are centered in the Bounding Box *(a)* will be centered on a path. Designs that are above or below center in the Bounding Box *(b)* will appear above or below the path they are applied to.

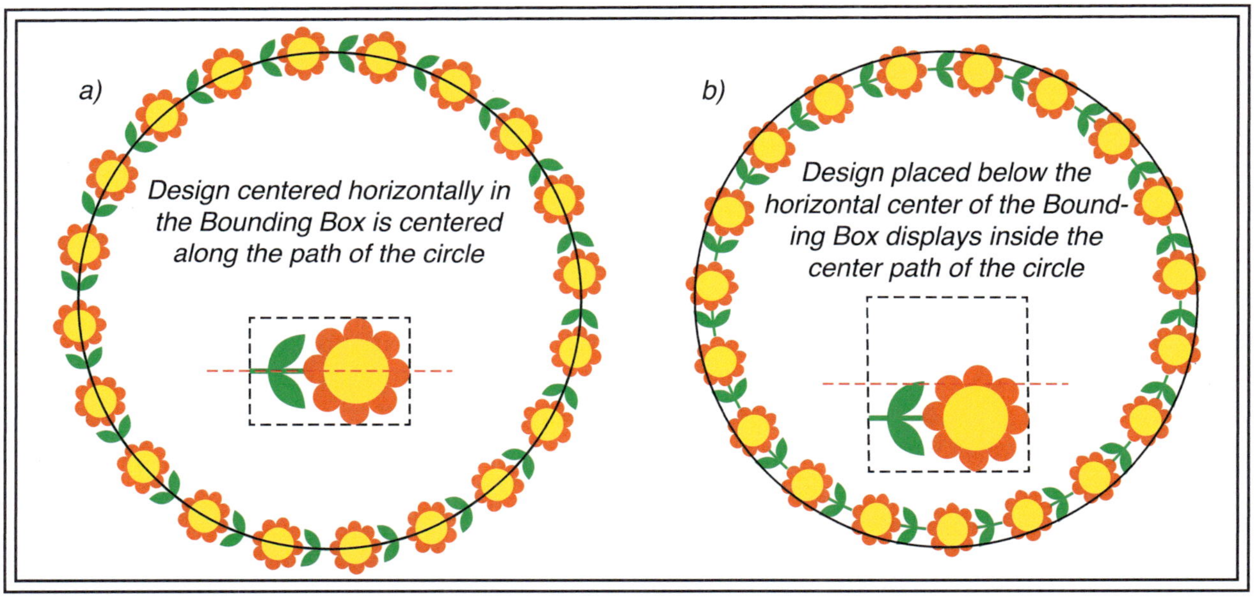

Bounding Boxes determine the placement of every part of a Pattern Brush. Learning how to piece the Bounding Boxes and design tiles together is what this book is all about.

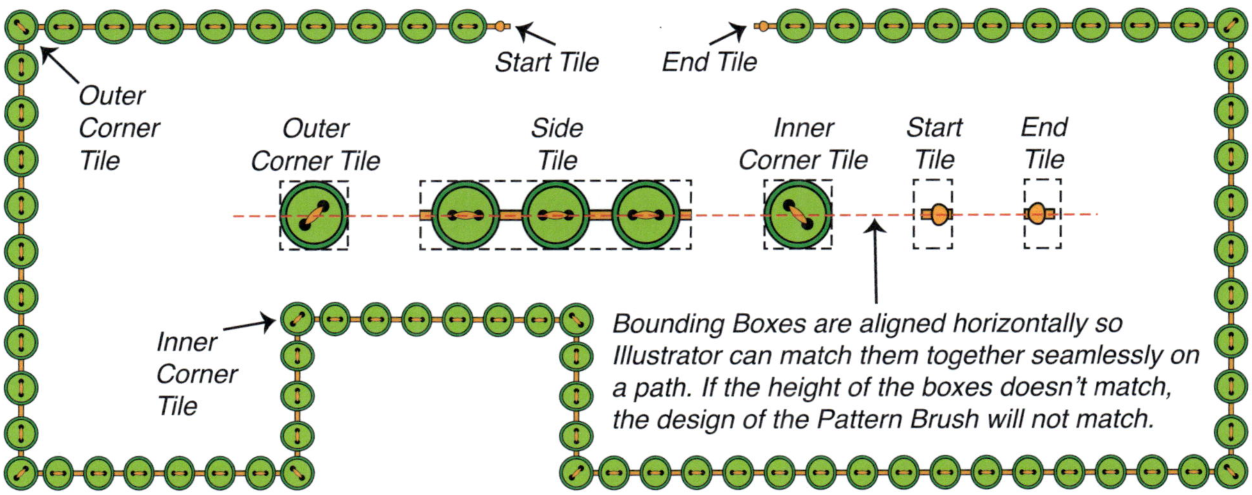

Tips and Time Savers

A working knowledge of Illustrator is suggested to master the techniques outlined in this book. Quality on-line training resources are available from a variety of sources. One of this author's favorite instructors is Deke McClelland, a leading teacher in the field of image editing and graphic design. Information on Deke's classes can be found on the Internet.

Action Keys and Shortcuts are different for a Mac® and a Microsoft® Windows® keyboard. This book is written using a Mac keyboard. Alternative keys for a PC are listed below.

Mac Keyboard	PC Keyboard
Command	Ctrl
Option	Alt

Turn Smart Guides on and leave them on. Smart Guides are visible when objects are created, moved or changed. They are snapping guides that assist with precision placement, alignment and movement of objects in relation to other objects and are valuable when it comes to making Tiles and Bounding Boxes fit together exactly. To turn Smart Guides on go to View>Smart Guides. To customize how Smart Guides function, go to Illustrator>Preferences>Smart Guides.

Outline Mode allows viewing of all lines and objects without the distraction of colors and fills. Combined with Smart Guides, Outline Mode makes precision designing and editing easier. Use this viewing mode when drawing Bounding Boxes, rotating tiles, and checking Pattern Brush tiles for accurate sizing and placement. Toggle in and out of Outline Mode by pressing Command+Y.

Bounding Boxes must have no Stroke color and no Fill color and be placed at the back layer of a design before it is moved to the Brushes Panel. **<u>The Bounding Boxes in this book have a black dashed line for illustration purposes only.</u>** To place a Bounding Box in the back layer, select the Bounding Box then go to Object>Arrange>Send to Back. The shortcut for that action is Shift+Command+[.

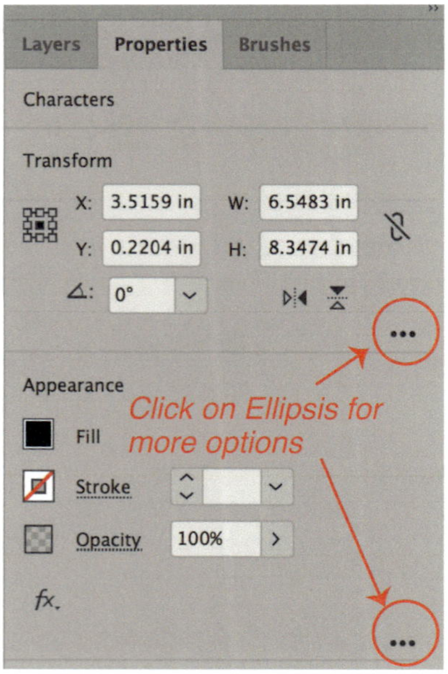

Streamline workflow by learning to navigate the **Essentials Workspace** located on the right side of the screen. It displays the most used tools in the Properties Panel based upon what is currently selected. An Ellipsis (...) indicates there are more click-able options available in a drop-down menu. Additional tools are available in the Toolbar on the left side of the screen and in the Window drop-down menu in the Toolbar at the top of the screen.

Add two other tabs to the Essentials Workspace: the **Layers Panel** and the **Brushes Panel.** Go to Window>Layers to open the Layers Panel and Window>Brushes to open the Brushes Panel. Click on the top of each Panel *(one at a time)* and drag them onto the Essentials Workspace next to Properties Tab. Click on the tabs to switch from one panel to the other.

Organize work in the Layers Panel. Create a new layer for each Pattern Brush by clicking on the ⊞ icon at the bottom of the Layers Panel. Layers are numbered in the order they are created. Double click on the text *(Layer 1, 2, 3, etc.)* to name the layer. Each object within the layer can be named in the same manner *(see example below)*. Think of a Layer as a File and the objects in the Layer as documents. Sometimes it is easier to select an object in the Layers Panel than on the artboard. To select an object in the Layers Panel, click on the small circle in the right column that is next to the **object's name**. To select the entire layer, click on the small circle in the right column that is next to the **layer's name**.

Objects are added to the top of a layer and display "on top" of other objects on the artboard. They can be moved on top of or behind other objects in the layer in two different ways.

1) **Select the object on the artboard**. Go to Object>Arrange and click either Bring to Front, Bring Forward, Send Backward or Send to Back.

2) **Select the object in the Layers Panel.** Drag it up or down to the desired placement. Changes made in the Layers Panel are immediately reflected on the artboard.

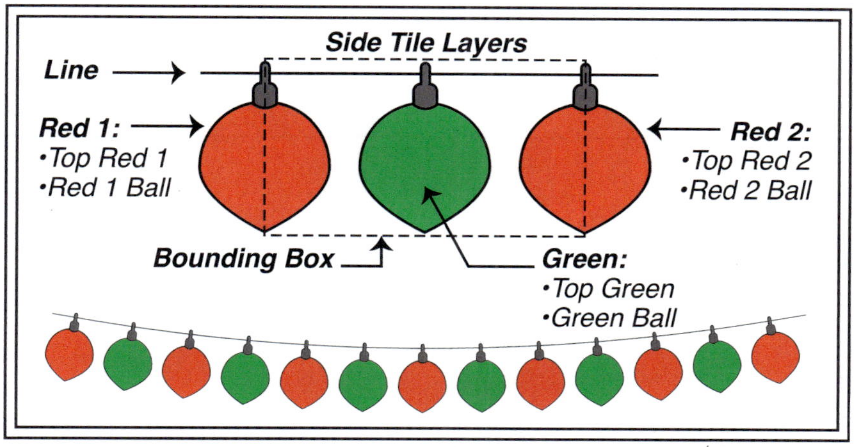

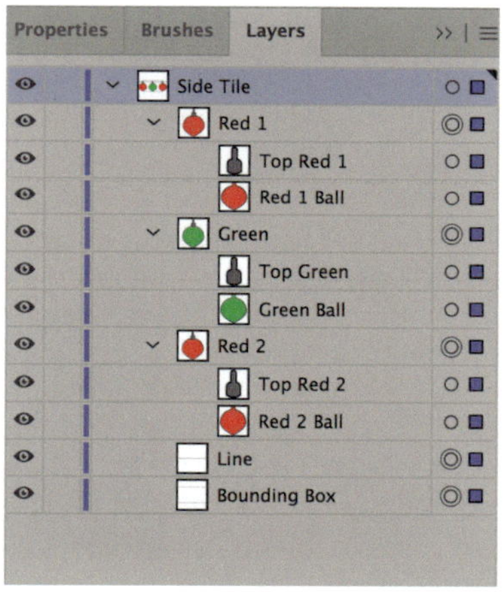

When an Object Can't Be a Pattern Brush

An error message is displayed if an object being drug into the Brushes Panel is prohibited. It never hurts to keep trying, but at the date of this publication, the following objects in Illustrator 24.2 must be modified before they can be used to create a Pattern Brush:

1) **A linked object or photograph** can't be used in a Pattern Brush until it has been embedded. With the object selected, go to the Properties Panel and click the Quick Actions Embed button.

2) **Text** can't be turned directly into a Pattern Brush. It must first be turned into outlines. For details, see Page 19.

3) **Objects with special effects, gradients or gradient meshes** cannot be used as a Pattern Brush unless they are rasterized. With the object selected go to Object>Rasterize. The object can then be used in a Pattern Brush, however it will no longer be vector art. If it is enlarged, it can lose quality due to pixelization.

Pattern Brush Tiles

(used in Pattern Brushes on the following page)

Outer Corner Tile

Side Tile

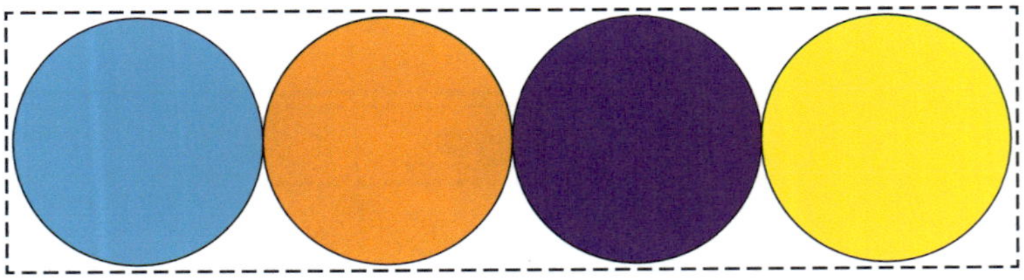

Side Tile

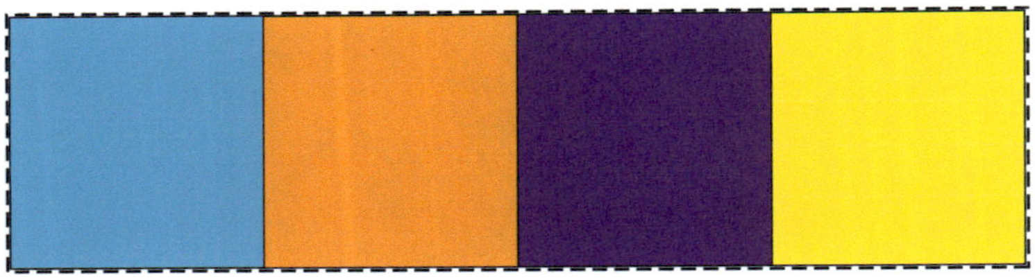

Side Tile

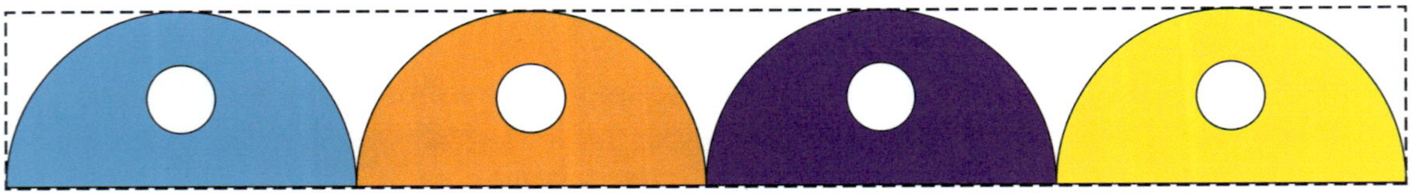

Creating Side Tiles

A Pattern Brush's Side Tile repeats on any straight or curved path it is applied to. Any other tiles added to the Pattern Brush must align and coordinate with the Side Tile.

Creating a Pattern Brush

1) **Create objects.** Create two or more objects. Assign them Fill and Stroke colors as desired.

2) **Align objects horizontally.** Select the objects. Go to the Align Panel. If it's not in the Essentials Workspace Toolbar, go to Window>Align to open it. Click on the icon to align the objects horizontally. Always create the Pattern Brush on the horizontal axis.

3) **Arrange and group objects together.** Use the arrow key to nudge objects next to each other. Select both objects and go to Object>Group or use the shortcut Command+G.

4) **Draw a Bounding Box** around the group of objects using the Rectangle Tool. The Bounding Box *(rectangle)* should be exactly as wide and high as the object group and have no Fill or Stroke color selected. It is important the Bounding Box is behind the objects. Select *only* the Bounding Box and go to Object>Arrange>Send to Back. When objects don't overlap or interlock, the Bounding Box may not be necessary. But when multiple tiles are used or specific spacing is desired, all tiles must be in Bounding Boxes.

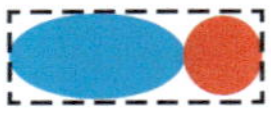

5) **Align and group objects.** Align objects and the Bounding Box vertically and horizontally. Group them together.

6) **Create a Pattern Brush.** Open the Brushes Panel. If it's not in the Toolbar, go to Window>Brushes to open it. Drag the newly created group to the Brushes Panel. A New Brush Dialogue Box will open. Select "Pattern Brush" and click OK.

7) **Name the Pattern Brush.** A Pattern Brush Options Dialogue Box opens next. Type a descriptive name for the brush in the Name field. Notice the grouped artwork appears in the second tile bin, called the Side Tile. It is the part of the Pattern Brush that repeats along any straight or curved line that doesn't have corners. The preview box shows what it will look like. Click OK.

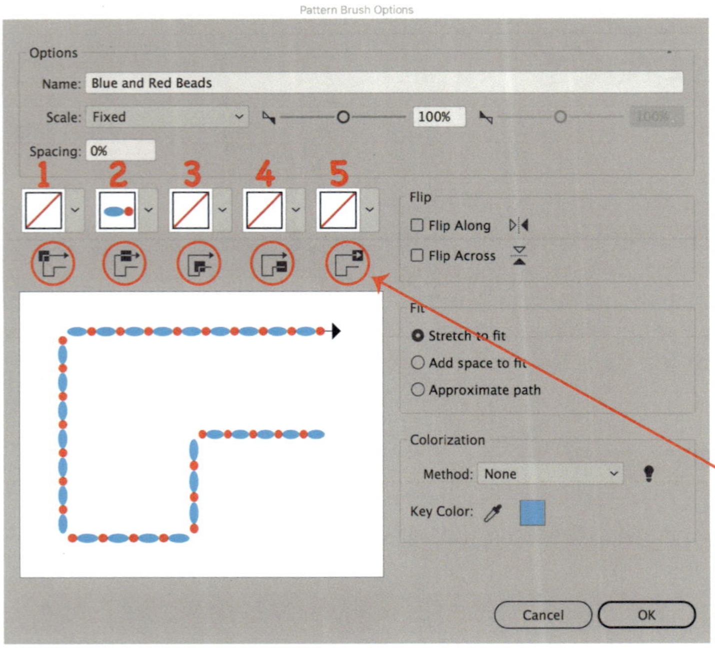

8) **Apply the Pattern Brush.** Create a line or object on the artboard and with it selected, click on the Pattern Brush in the Brushes Panel.

Tile Bins for Illustrator 24.2

1 - Outer Corner Tile
2 - Side Tile
3 - Inner Corner Tile
4 - Start Tile
5 - End Tile

In earlier versions of Illustrator, the tile bins are in a different order. Identify them by the diagrams located below them. The red numbers are added for illustration purposes and won't be on the screen.

Single Object Side Tiles

Single Object Side Tiles are simple to make and useful in many ways. Begin by creating an object. Draw a Bounding Box around it and group both together. Drag the group into the Brushes Panel. Experiment with different Fills, Strokes and with black and white. Black and white Pattern Brushes work well for doodle art projects and when creating coloring books. Edit the value of the Stroke in the Properties Panel to resize the Pattern Brush on a path.

TIP: When making a black and white Pattern Brush, a "no Fill" selection will make the pattern brush transparent. Fill the object with white to prevent an illustration's background from showing through the patterned line.

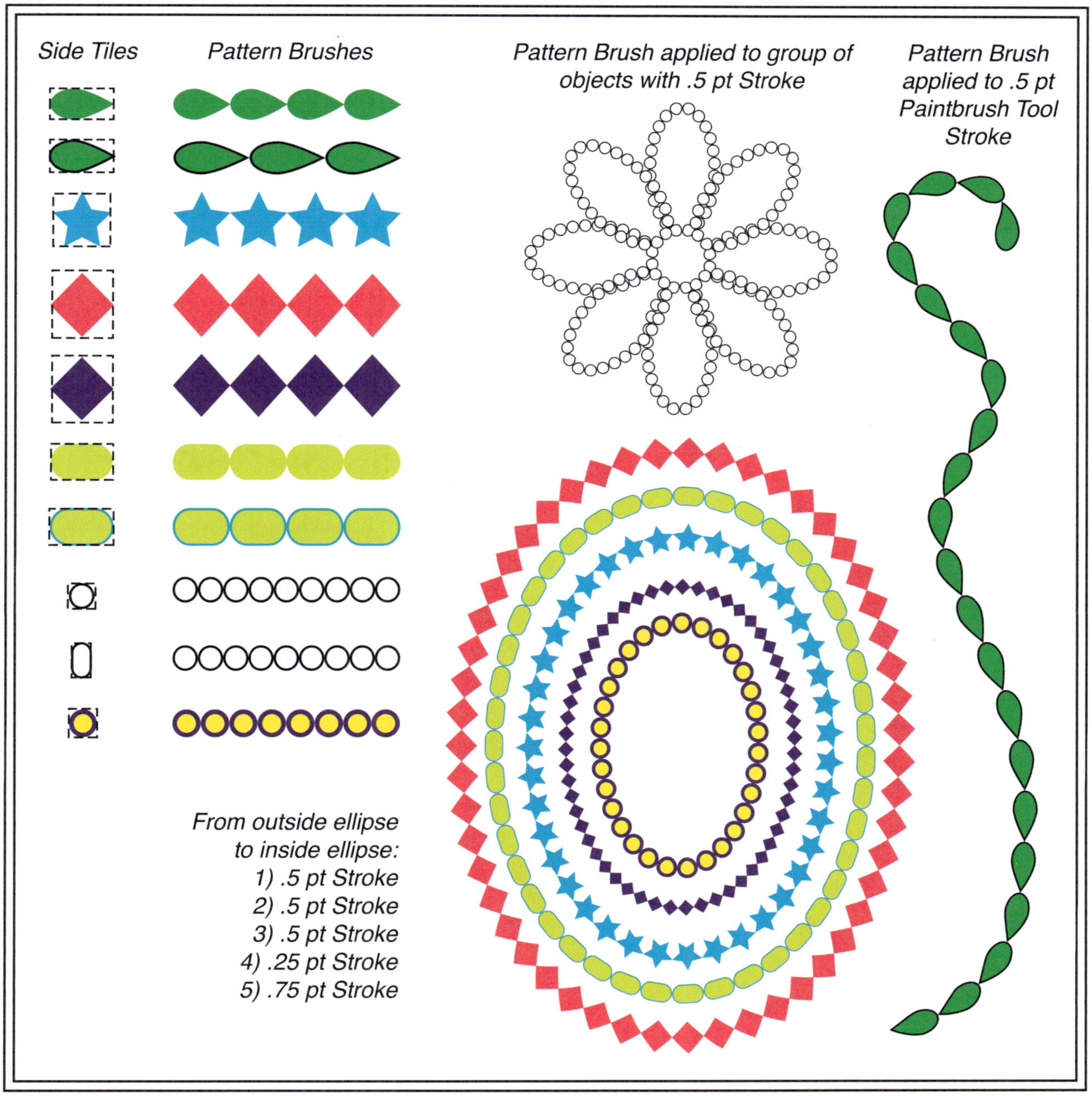

Multiple Object Side Tiles

There is no limit to the number of Pattern Brushes that can be created by combining multiple objects in a design. Tiles can include combinations of different shapes, sizes and colors. The key is to align all objects horizontally so the repeating patterns appear seamless. Once objects are aligned, create and place a Bounding Box around them, send the Bounding Box to the back, group everything and create a new Pattern Brush as described on Page 16.

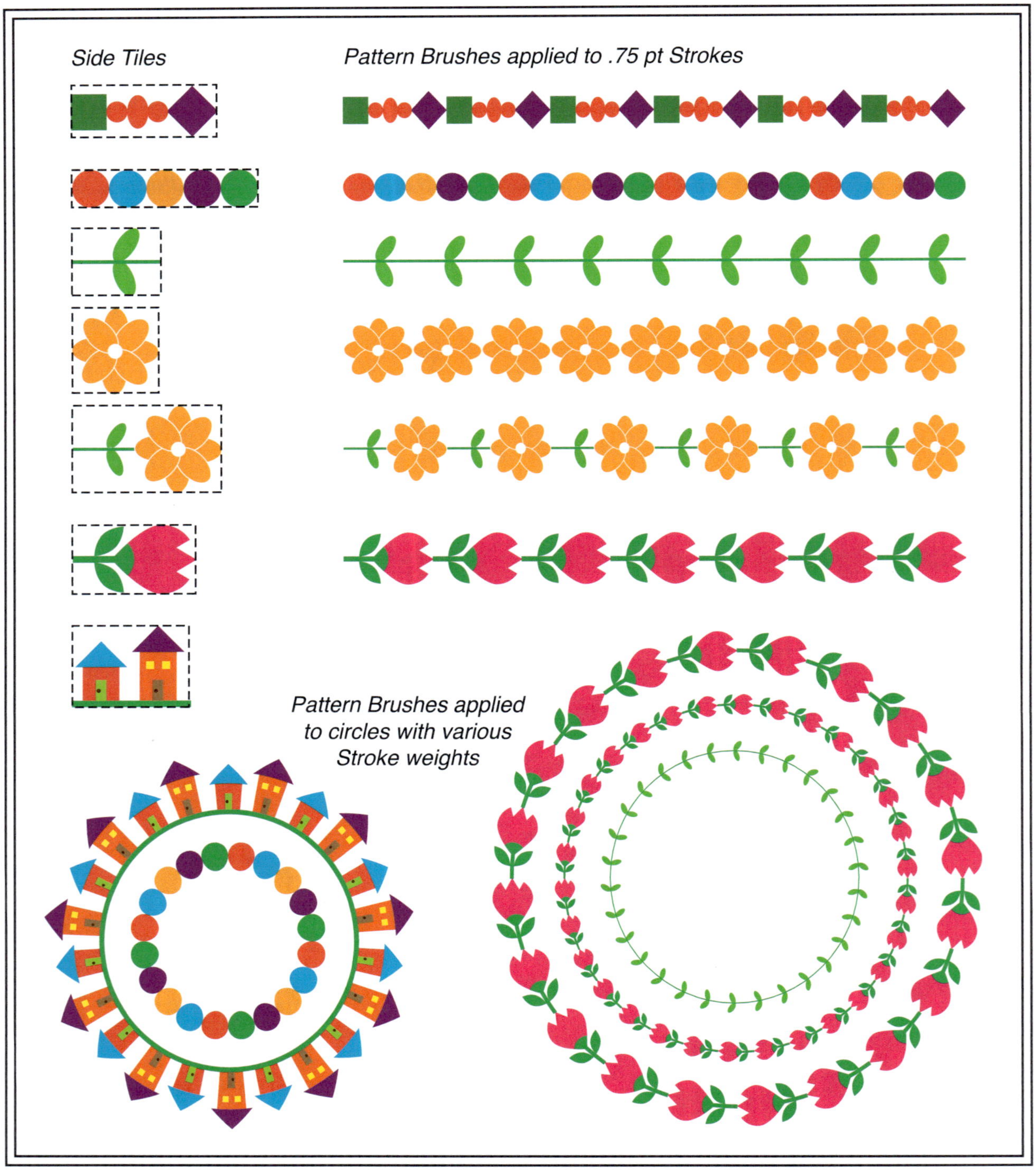

Text Side Tiles

Letters and symbols of any size, color or combination can be used to create Pattern Brushes, but they must first be converted from fonts to outlines. Once they are converted, they can even be combined with traditional objects such as the heart and text in the example below. The process is simple.

1) **Type the text and select it.** A solid line will appear under the letters.

2) **Create Outlines.** Go to Type>Create Outlines. If the Create Outlines option is grayed out, the text is not selected. By clicking on Create Outlines, the text is automatically converted to outlines and will be treated as a group of objects. To edit or move letters individually, ungroup the objects.

TIP: When text is selected, there is a Quick Action Button in the Properties Panel *(in the Essentials Workspace)*. Click on Create Outlines to convert text to objects.

3) Drag the letters into the Brushes Panel to create a Pattern Brush *(see page 16)*.

The fastest and simplest way to evenly space text and objects in a Pattern Brush is to adjust the spacing in the Pattern Brush Options Dialogue Box either when the Pattern Brush is created or later, by double clicking on the Pattern Brush in the Brushes Panel. Draw a design, adjust the spacing between each of its objects, group and drag the objects into the Brushes Panel to create a Pattern Brush. When the Pattern Brush Options Dialogue Box opens, enter a percentage value in the Spacing option. That percentage of space will be placed between each of the repeating Side Tiles *(but not between the objects IN the Side Tile)*. No Bounding Boxes are needed. Start with 5-10% and click OK to view. Edit as desired to adjust spacing. A larger percentage increases the spacing between letters while a smaller percentage decreases the space.

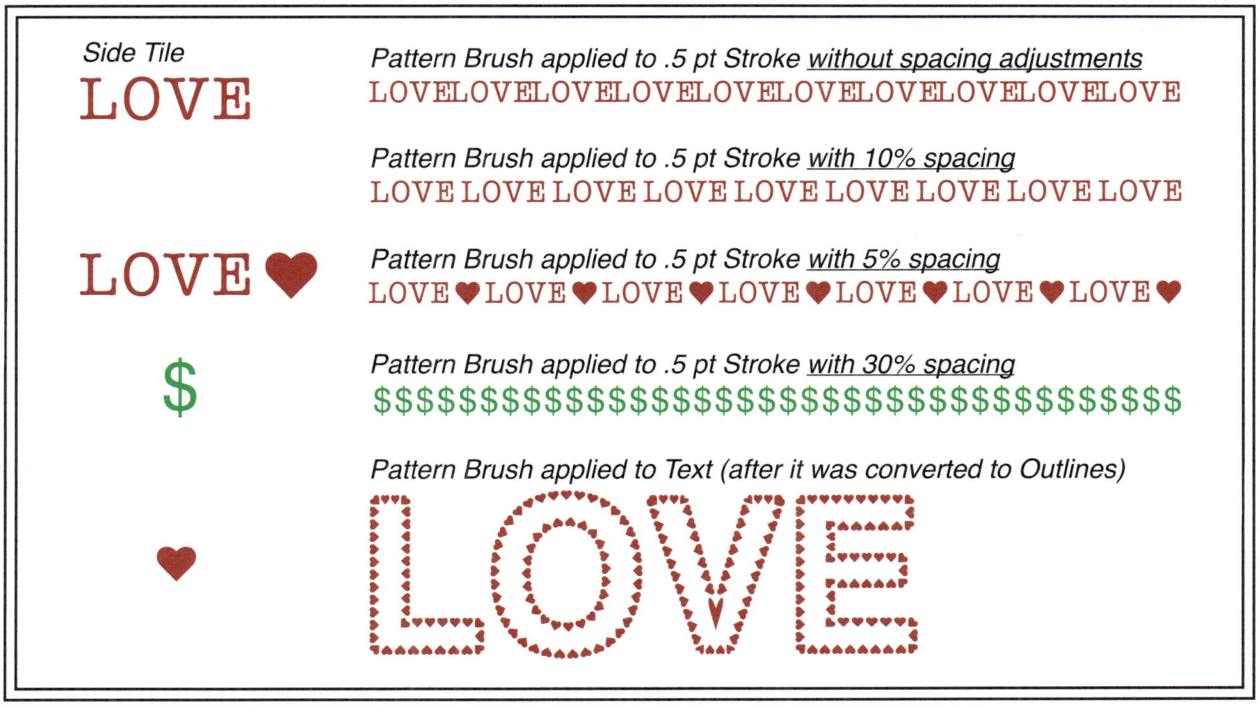

Overlapping Seamless Side Tiles

Not all Pattern Brushes are created equal. A pattern repeats from the outermost point of its left and right sides. If two overlapping circles *(a)* are placed in the Brushes Panel without any further formatting, the Pattern Brush will not have a continuous seamless overlap as seen below *(b)*.

Overlapping designs require precision and a Bounding Box. The following process works for object groups that have a Fill Color but NO Stroke color:

1) **Create a design and group all objects together.** Go to View>Smart Guides to turn on Smart Guides. Draw the design. With the objects selected, press Command+G.

2) **Make a copy.** Command+Shift+Drag to the right to add a horizontal copy. Overlap the two groups with the spacing desired for the pattern repeat *(c)*.

3) **Group the design groups together.** Select objects and press Command+G.

4) **Switch to Outline View.** Go to View>Outline or use the shortcut Command+Y to toggle in and out of Outline View. Use this view to make sure spacing is precise.

5) **Place a Bounding Box** around the object group where the pattern is to be repeated *(d)*. In the example below, the desired effect is to have a blue/red overlap. To accomplish this, place the left side of the Bounding Box in the center of the left blue circle and the right side of the Bounding Box in the center of the right blue circle. When the pattern repeats, the two half blue circles meet seamlessly, creating a red/blue overlapping Pattern Brush.

6) **Format Bounding Box.** Remove Stroke and Fill Colors from the Bounding Box. With Bounding Box selected, go to Object>Arrange>Send to Back. Select all objects and group together.

7) **Create Pattern Brush.** Select the grouped objects and Bounding Box *(e)* and drag them into the Brushes Panel. Test the Pattern Brush by applying it to a path *(f)*. If the spacing isn't quite right, edit and try again.

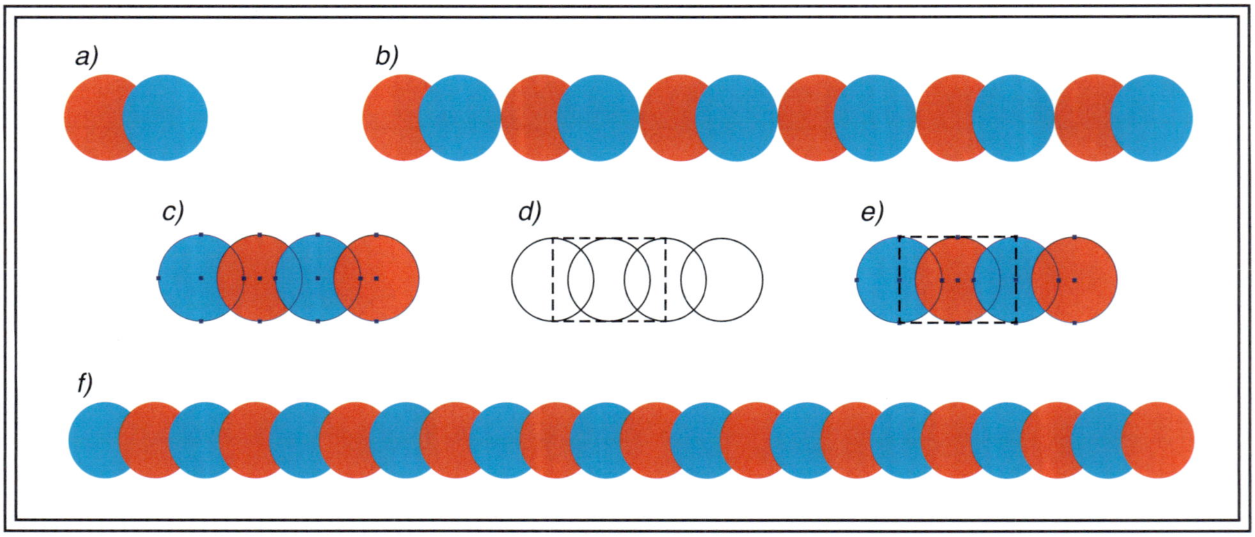

Interlocking Seamless Side Tiles

Side Tiles can be designed to have a seamless interlocking or overlapping flow. The following process works for object groups that have a Fill Color but NO Stroke Color.

1) **Turn on Smart Guides.** Go to View>Smart Guides.

2) **Create design.** Draw a 2" black line with 10 pt Stroke. With it selected, go to Effect>Distort & Transform. Select Zig Zag. Dialogue Box Options: Size 0.2", Absolute, 3 Ridges Per Segment and Smooth. Command+Shift+Drag to the right to **create a copy** on the same horizontal line. Give the second line a red Stroke. Convert both lines to Objects. Go to Object>Path>Outline Stroke.

3) **Overlap the objects.** Select the left object. Drag a Guide from the workspace's left ruler to mark the centers of its lower curves *(a)*. Shift+Drag the red object left until its left side intersects with the black Object's left lower curve *(b)*.

4) **Add a Bounding Box.** Toggle in and out of Outline Mode *(Command+Y)* for precision. Use the Rectangle Tool to surround the Object group for the pattern repeat. The Guides mark the side boundaries; the top and bottom should intersect with the upper and lower boundaries of the objects *(c)*. The Bounding Box should have no Fill or Stroke color and must be moved to the back of the group before the next step. Spacing must be exact.

5) **Remove extra pieces.** With everything selected, click on the Divide Pathfinder Tool. Next, ungroup everything by pressing Shift+Command+G. Use the Direct Selection Tool *(Keyboard Shortcut A)* to select and delete the pieces outside of the Bounding Box *(d)*.

6) **Complete the interlock design.** Select the small red segment that overlaps the black object on the right *(e)* and change its color to black *(f)*. Switch back to the Selection Tool *(Keyboard Shortcut V)*. Group objects and Bounding Box *(Keyboard Shortcut Command+G)*.

7) **Create the Pattern Brush.** Select the group and drag it into the Brushes Panel *(g)*.

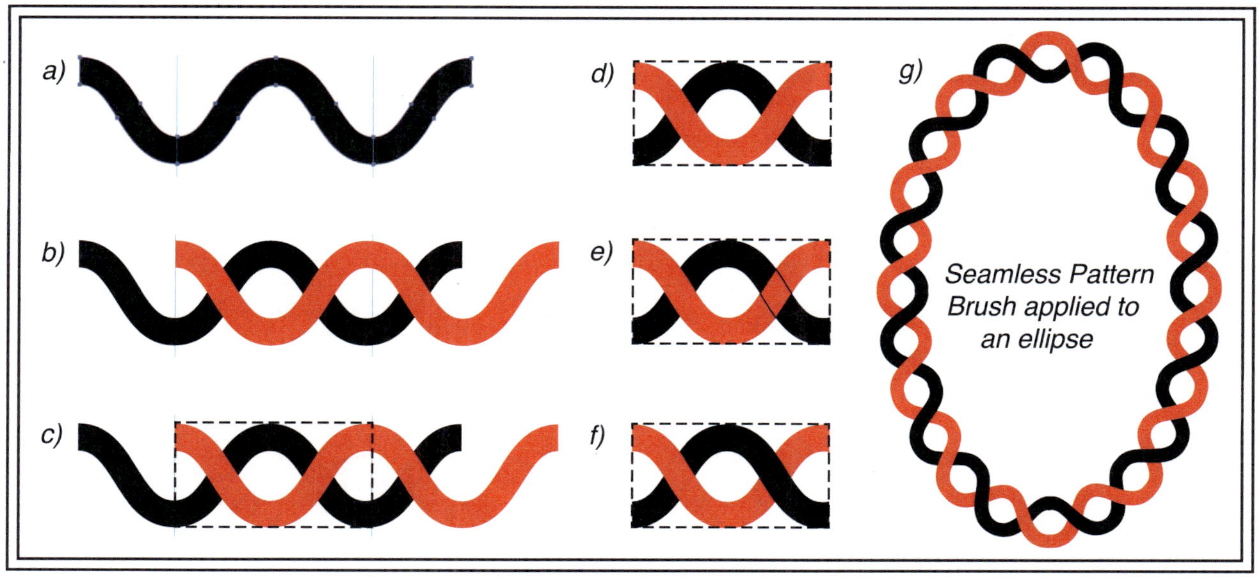

Seamless Side Tiles with Color Stroke

It requires more steps to add an object with a Stroke color to a Pattern Brush so that the Strokes don't appear between every repeat of the design. The process below describes how:

Example of an improperly formatted Pattern Brush. A vertical Stroke appears between each repeat of the objects.

1) **Turn on Smart Guides.** Go to View>Smart Guides.

2) **Create design.** Draw a 4" red line with a 15 pt Stroke. With the line selected, go to Effect>Distort and select Transform>ZigZag. Dialogue Box Options: Size .25, Absolute, Ridges Per Segment 5, Points Smooth, OK.

3) **Convert line to outlines.** With the line selected, go to Object>Path>Outline Stroke.

4) **Add Stroke.** With outlined object selected, add 2 pt black Stroke.

5) **Make a copy.** Command+Shift+Drag to the right to create a copy on the same horizontal axis. Change the Fill Color of the duplicated object to blue. Hold down the Shift key and drag the blue object on top of the red object, evenly staggering their upper and lower ridges *(a)*.

6) **Expand.** With the two objects selected, go to Object>Expand. Make sure Fill and Stroke are Selected in the Expand Dialogue Box. Click OK.

7) **Switch to Outline View.** Go to View>Outline for the most accurate view to align the objects.

8) **Place a Bounding Box** around the object group where the pattern is to be repeated *(b)*. Bounding Box should have no Stroke or Fill Color. Send it to the back before the next step.

9) **Remove Extra Pieces.** With everything selected, click on the Divide Pathfinder Tool. Select all again and ungroup by pressing Shift+Command+G. Use the Direct Selection Tool to select any pieces outside of the Bounding Box and delete them. Do NOT delete the Bounding Box *(c)*.

10) **Group all and exit Outline View.** Select all objects and press Command+G to group all objects together. Press Command+Y to exit Outline View.

11) **Create Pattern Brush.** Drag the objects into the Brushes Panel. Apply to a path to test it *(d)*.

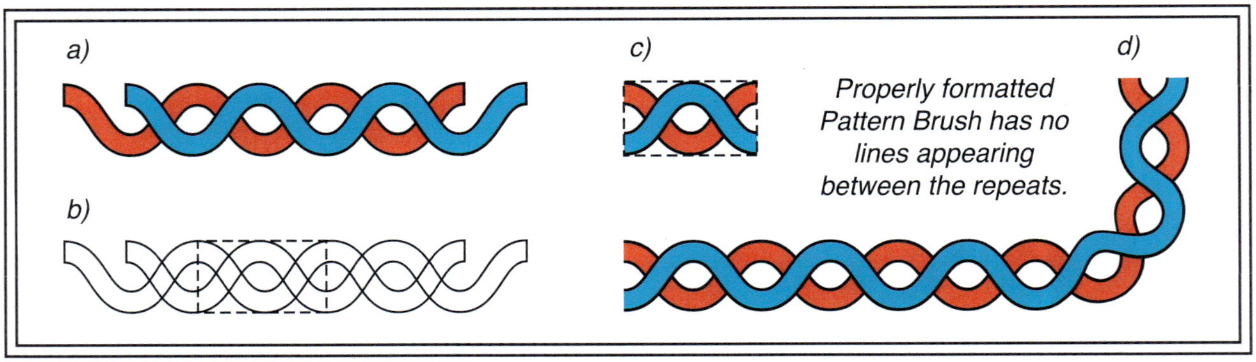

Creating Doodle Art Side Tiles

Doodle Art is an organic hand-drawn design style. Pattern Brushes made from Doodle Art are whimsical and fun to create. With a few simple tips, a Doodle Art Pattern Brush can be simple and quick to make, possessing all the characteristics of a seamless repeating pattern.

1) **Create a design on the horizontal axis.** If the design includes an actual line, the anchor points on both ends must be the same size and aligned exactly *(or you will have to edit them)*. Try this simple method: print a page of 3" wide black lines with a 2 pt thickness on white paper. Draw the Doodle Art on the printed line with a fine point black marker.

2) **Scan the artwork** using a traditional scanner or one of the many scanning apps available online. Save as a .jpg, .png, .tif or .pdf file. Drag the artwork into Illustrator.

3) **Format and clean up the design.** Follow these steps:

- Select the artwork and go to Object>Transform>Scale. Resize it to fit on the artboard. The horizontal line MUST be exactly horizontal for ends to match. Adjust if necessary.
- Select artwork and go to Object>Image Trace>Make and Expand.
- Ungroup *(Shift+Command+G)* and with artwork still selected, go to Select>Inverse.
- Using the Magic Wand Tool *(Keyboard Shortcut Y)*, click on the white area around the design and press delete to remove all the surrounding white. Only the black vector lines will remain.
- Ungroup *(Shift+Command+G)* and edit the design as desired. Shorten ends as needed to achieve the right spacing for the pattern repeat.
- Add a Bounding Box and drag the design into the Brushes Panel.

4) **Test the pattern.** Draw an oval and apply the Pattern Brush to the path. Inspect the repeats and make adjustments if needed.

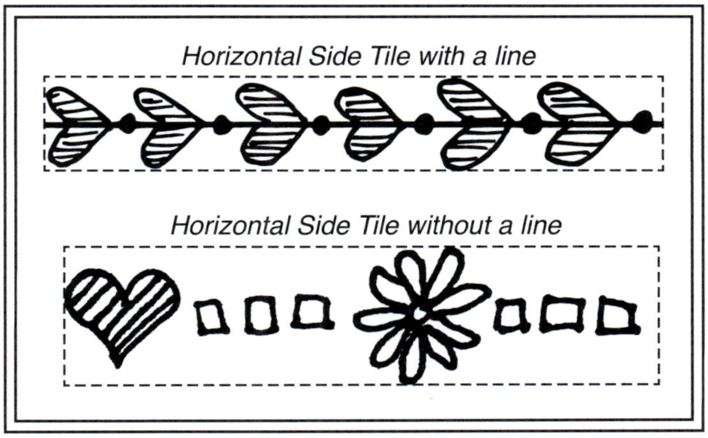

Doodle Art is usually black but it can be any color. In the Brushes Panel, choose the Tints Option under Colorization. Edit Stroke color in the Properties Panel.

Pattern Brush Tiles

(used in Pattern Brushes on the following page)

Side Tile

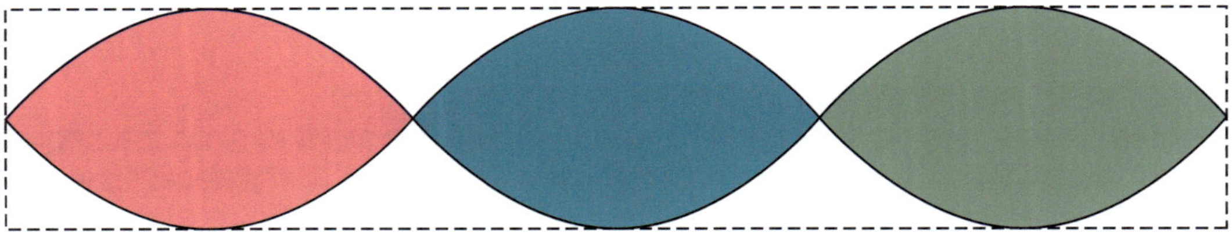

Side Tile

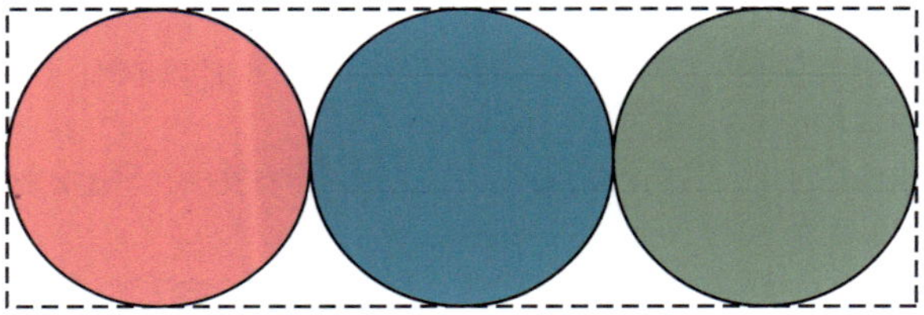

Outer Corner Tile

Side Tile

Side Tile

Creating Corner Tiles

Corner Tiles allow the Pattern Brush to have a smooth and seamless transition around corners. Some paths have both an Inner and an Outer Corner.

Auto Generated Corner Tiles

Corner Tiles provide a smooth transition for a Pattern Brush when a path changes direction. **Beginning with Illustrator CC**, four tile options are automatically generated for both Outer and Inner Corners of a Pattern Brush based upon the Side Tile's original artwork.

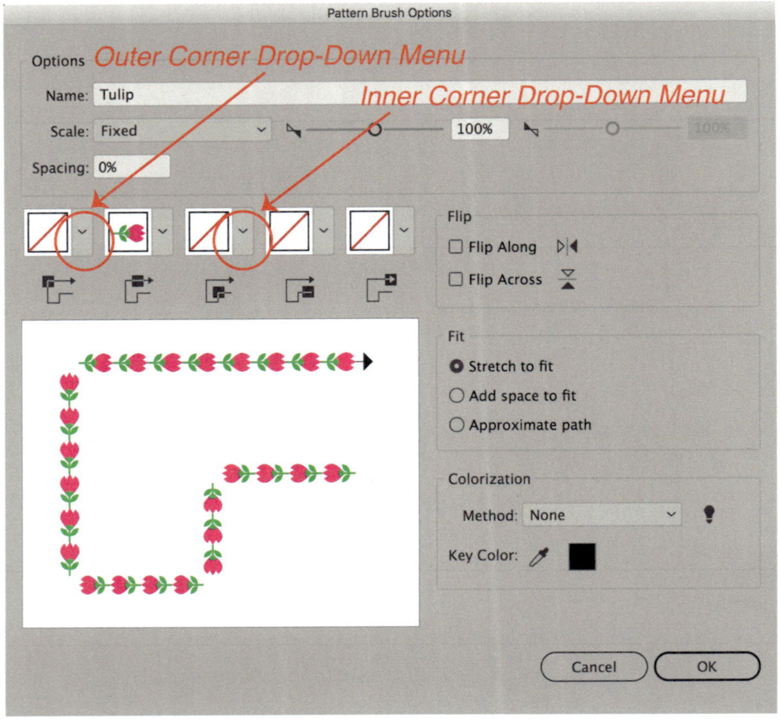

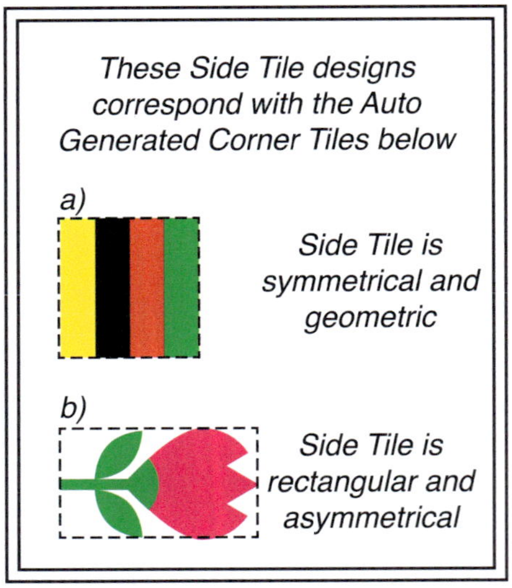

The options are displayed in drop-down menus next to the tile bins in the Pattern Brush Options Dialogue Box *(see above)*. Auto Generated Corner Tiles resulting from symmetrical and/or geometric Side Tiles *(a)* can often be used "as is", but Auto Generated Corner Tiles originating from asymmetrical shaped Side Tiles *(b)* may not be usable. This is how the four corner choices are generated:

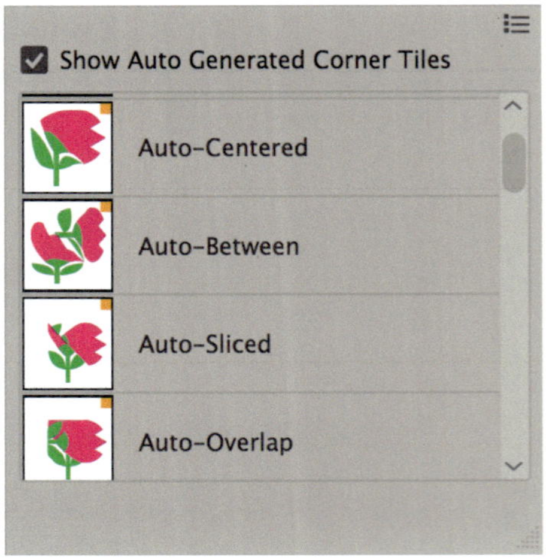

Auto-Centered - Side Tile stretches around the corner and is centered.

Auto-Between - Two Side Tiles are moved all the way into the corner and then are stretched to fit.

Auto-Sliced - Side Tile is sliced diagonally and mitered into the corner.

Auto-Overlap - Two Side Tiles are overlapped in the corner.

It is always worth previewing the Auto Generated Tiles before spending time reinventing the wheel!

Making an Outer Corner Tile

An Outer Corner Tile fits into the corner where the **bottom part** of two adjacent Bounding Boxes makes a 90° angle. Always create the Outer Corner Tile to fit in the top left corner of a rectangle. Illustrator will adjust the direction of the other corners.

1) **Turn Smart Guides on**. Go to View>Smart Guides.

2) **Create the Side Tile.** Draw a design. Add a Bounding Box *(a)* and group the items together.

3) **Duplicate the design.** Press Command+Shift and drag to the right until Smart Guides displays the word "Intersect". A copy of the original design group is placed exactly next to the original design. The two designs must intersect for the rest of the process to work properly.

4) **Rotate the left Side Tile 90°.** Select the left Side Tile. Press the keyboard letter R *(Keyboard shortcut for Rotate)*. A small blue circle appears in its center *(c)*. Click on the left Side Tile's **BOTTOM** right corner *(d)*. This moves the blue circle to that corner and is where the rotation needs to occur. With the left tile selected, hold down the Shift key and drag the left tile 90° to rotate it *(e)*. Switch to Outline Mode and check corners for precision *(Command+Y)*.

5) **Create a Bounding Box and design for the Outer Corner Tile.** Using the Rectangle Tool, draw a Bounding Box to fit in the corner opening between the two Side Tiles *(f)*. Create a design to fit inside the Bounding Box. It does not have to FILL the box but it can *(g)*. Toggle in and out of Outline View to make sure corners are precise. Remove the Stroke and Fill color from Bounding Box and send it to the back. Group the Outer Tile and its Bounding Box together and follow directions for Adding Corner Tiles to the Brushes Panel on Page 30.

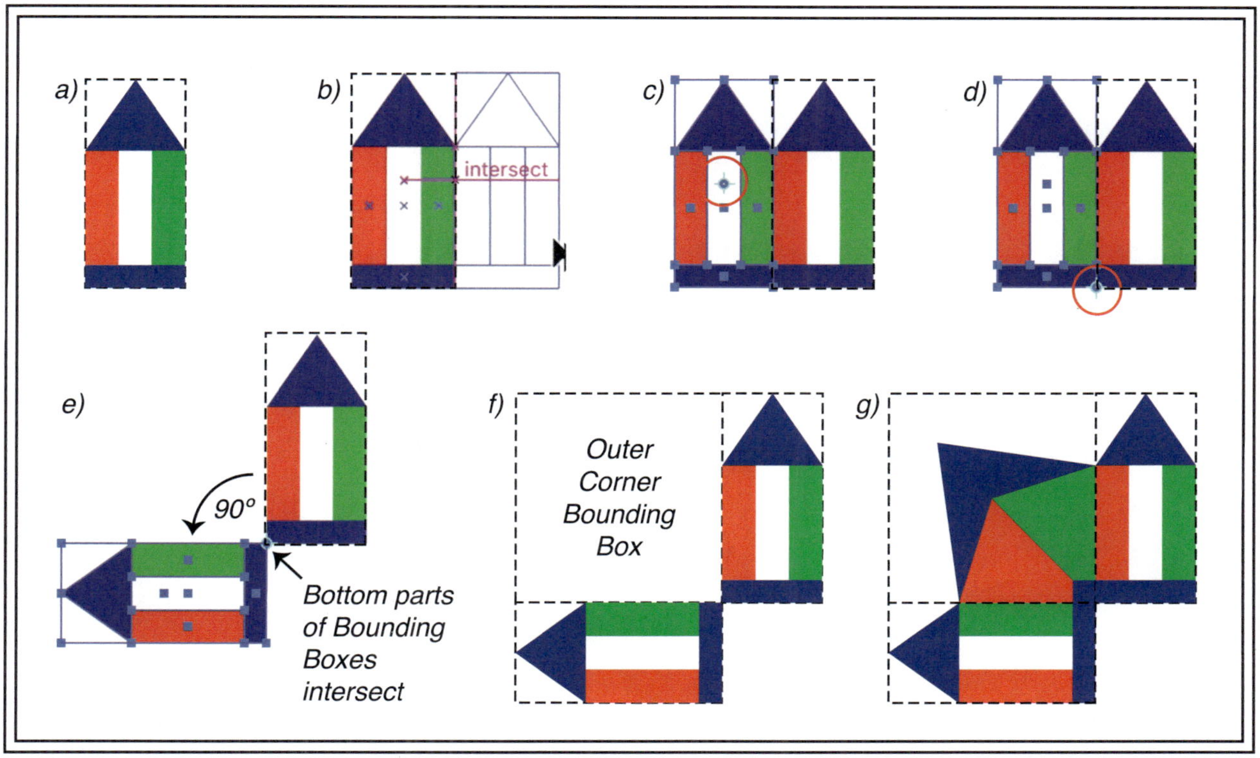

Making an Inner Corner Tile

An Inner Corner Tile fits into the corner where the **top part** of two adjacent Bounding Boxes makes a 90° angle. Follow the steps below to create the Inner Corner Tile. Make it to fit the lower right angle shown below *(e)*. Illustrator will adjust the direction of all other corners.

1) **Duplicate the design.** Using the Side Tile example from the previous page, select the Side Tile and Command+Shift+Drag the Side Tile and its Bounding Box to the right until the copy is exactly next to the first tile *(a)*. Smart Guides displays the word "Intersect" when the duplicate is in place.

2) **Rotate the right Side Tile 90°.** Select the right Side Tile. Press the keyboard letter R *(shortcut for Rotate)*. A small blue circle appears in the center of the design *(b)*. Click on the **TOP** left corner of the right Side Tile. This moves the blue circle to that corner and is where the rotation needs to occur *(c)*. With the right tile selected, hold down the Shift key and drag the right tile 90° to rotate it *(d)*. Switch to Outline Mode to check corners for precision *(Command+Y)*.

3) **Create a Bounding Box and design for the Inner Corner Tile.** Using the Rectangle Tool, draw a Bounding Box to fit in the corner opening between the two Side Tiles *(e)*. Create a design to fit inside the Bounding Box. It does not have to FILL the box but it can *(f)*. Toggle in and out of Outline View *(Command+Y)* as needed.

4) **Rotate the Inner Corner Tile 180°.** This rotation is required because Illustrator flips the Inner Corner Tile as it goes into the Brushes Panel. Remove the Stroke and Fill color from the Bounding Box, send the Bounding Box the back, group the Inner Corner and Bounding Box together and follow directions for adding Corner Tiles to the Brushes Panel on Page 30.

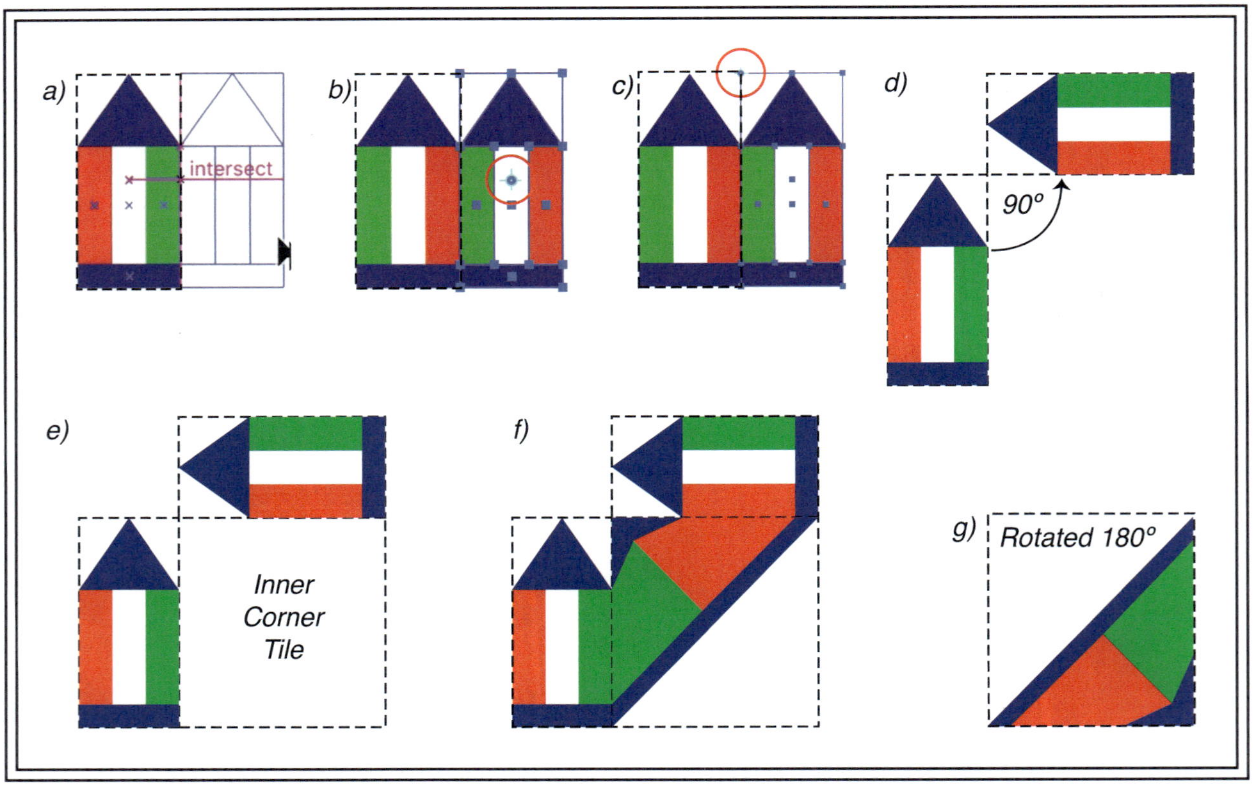

Editing Auto Generated Corner Tiles

Using Auto Generated tiles for the corners is always worth considering. Some of the Auto Generated tiles are beautiful and can be used "as is" or with minimal tweaking.

1) **Select an Outer Corner Tile** from the Auto Generated options *(see page 26)* and click OK.

2) **Drag the Pattern Brush onto the artboard** from the Brushes Panel and ungroup the tiles. Begin editing the corner tile as desired. Use caution to preserve the parts of the design that match with the Side Tile of the Pattern Brush; make sure the Bounding Box is behind all layers.

3) **Drag the edited tile back into the Brushes Panel.** Hold down the Option key and drag the edited tile back into the Brushes Panel into its proper tile location. <u>If the Corner Tile and Side Tile are not the same height</u>, you must a) remove the Side Tile's original Bounding Box, b) create a new Bounding Box for the Side Tile that is the same height as the Corner Tile's Bounding Box, and c) drag BOTH tiles back into the Brushes Panel. NOTE: These editing instructions will not work if there are clipping masks on the Auto-Generated Corner Tile, as many more steps are involved.

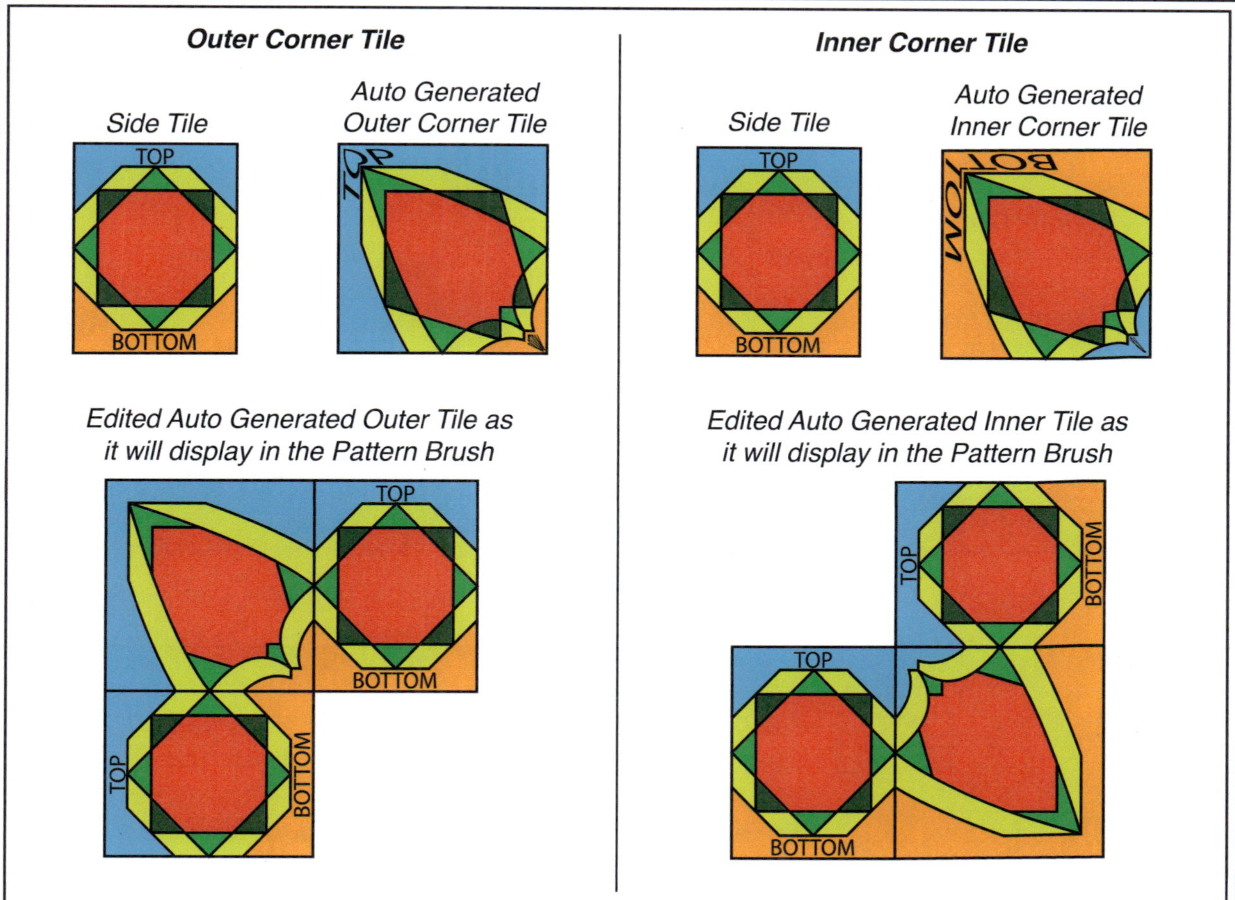

The edits on both of the Auto Generated Tiles were similar. Using the Selection Tool, both the lettering and the squiggly lines in the corners were selected and deleted. Some pieces were joined together using the Pathfinder Tool and then recolored. The basic shape of the design was preserved and flows seamlessly into the Side Tiles.

Adding Corner Tiles to the Brushes Panel

The Simplest Method of adding Corner Tiles into the Brushes Panel is to drag them in.

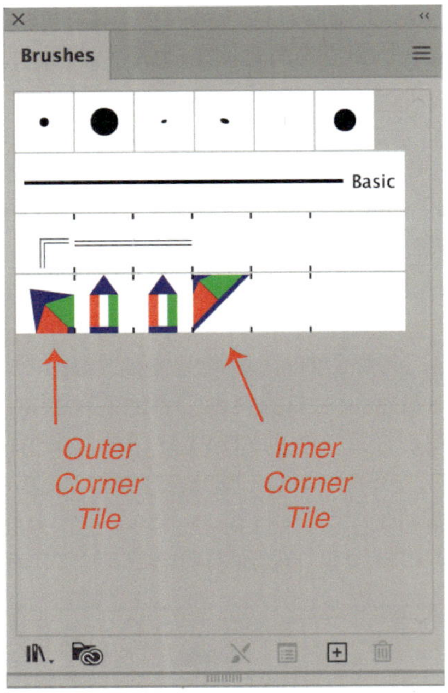

1) **Add Outer Corner Tile** - Open the Brushes Panel. Select the grouped design with its Bounding Box, hold down the Option Key and drag it to the Outer Corner Tile's Position.

2) **Add Inner Corner Tile** - Open the Brushes Panel. Select the grouped design with its Bounding Box, hold down the Option Key and drag it to the Inner Corner Tile's Position.

3) **Preview the Results** - The preview pane in the Pattern Brush Options Dialogue Box displays both the Outer Corner Tile and the Inner Corner Tile on a path. If a tile doesn't fit properly or if another look is desired, make adjustments and try again.

Adding an Edited Corner Tile - Hold down the Option Key and drag the new tile on top of the old one in the Brushes Panel.

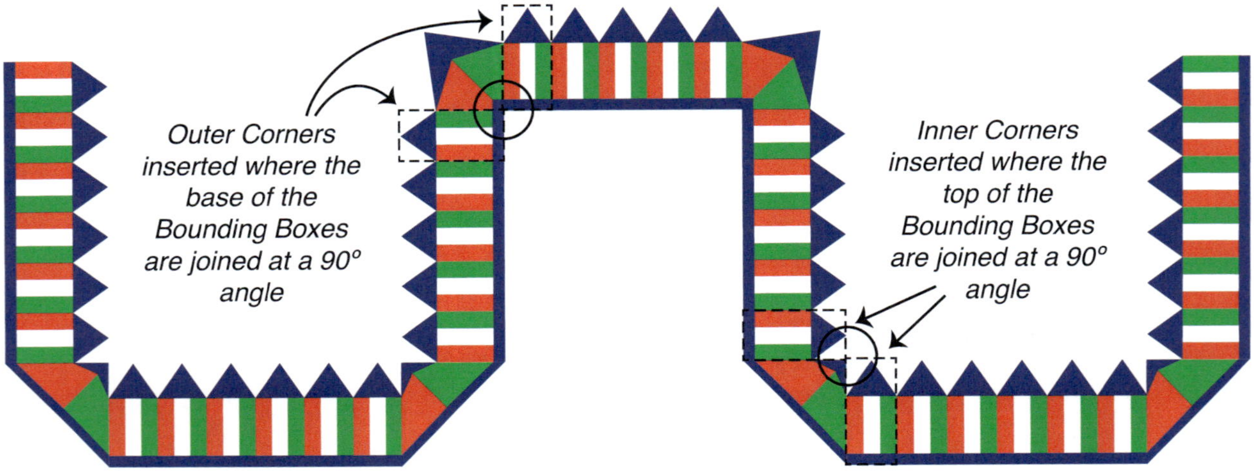

Use the Swatches Panel When Simple Doesn't Work

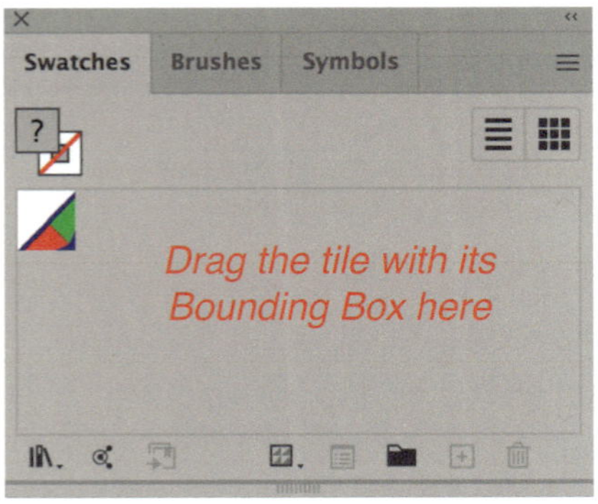

If a design will not drag into the Brushes Panel, go to Window>Swatches and **drag it into the Swatches Panel**. This places it in the drop-down menus of the Brushes Panel where the Auto Generated Tiles are located *(see Page 26).*

Open the Brushes Panel. Go to the Outer or Inner Corner Tile bin and click on the drop-down menu. Any designs added into the Swatches Panel will appear as numbered New Swatches. Click on one to select it. This method can be used to add any new tiles to the Brushes Panel.

Think Outside the Box

The corners of Pattern Brushes are typically drawn within the confines of a square Bounding Box. However, **they can actually exist outside of the box**. The key is to use the same size Bounding Box that would be used for a traditional sized Outer Corner Tile. Place the larger design on top of the Bounding Box. Illustrator uses the Bounding Box as the guide, but allows the larger part of the design to flow outside of its bounds and sit on TOP of the repeating Side Tiles. The examples below show Outer Corner Tiles that overlap the boundaries of their Bounding Box.

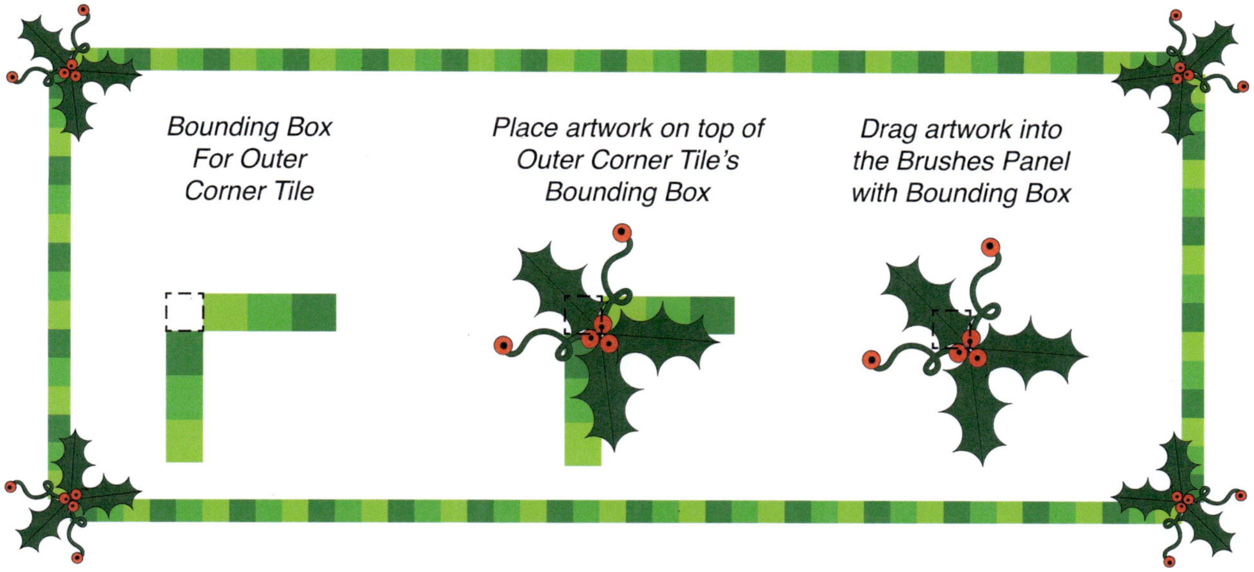

Drawing outside the box does have its limits but the only way to know whether or not a design can be used is to try it. Sometimes tweaking the size or slightly shifting the artwork is all it takes to fit an oversized Outer Corner Tile into a Pattern Brush. Also, when different sizes are being tried, it is easy to accidentally move or resize the Bounding Box. That alone will prevent the Outer Corner Tile from being placed properly. If nothing seems to work, make sure the Bounding Box is placed right in relation to the artwork and that it is at the back of the artwork layers.

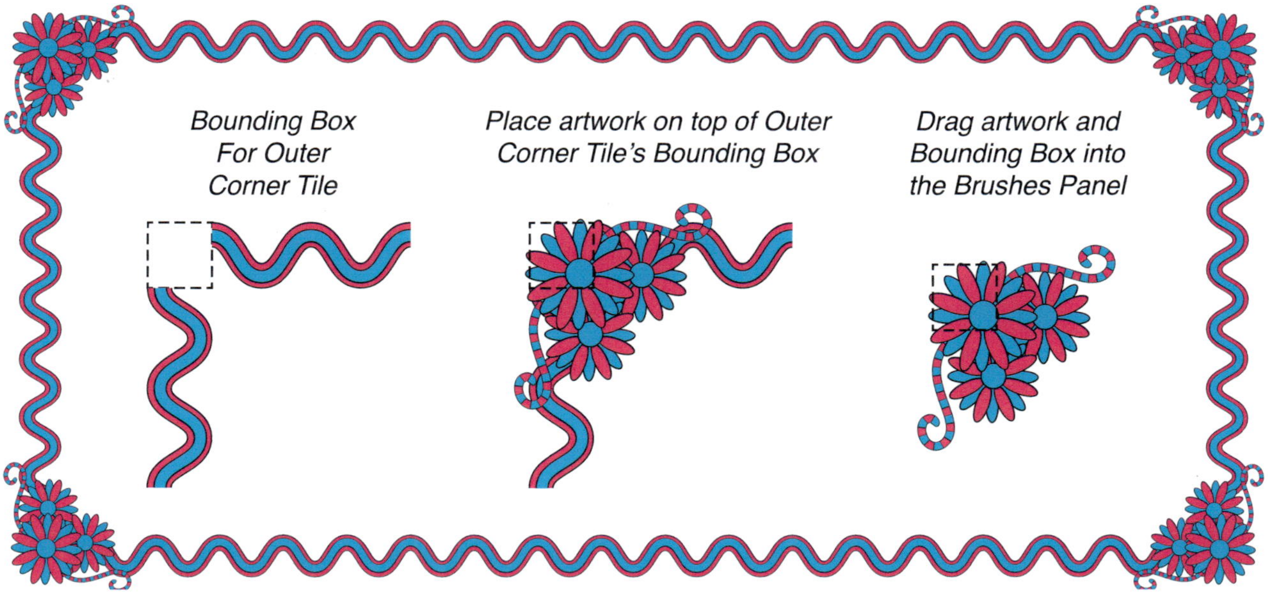

Pattern Brush Tiles

(used in Pattern Brushes on the following page)

Side Tile

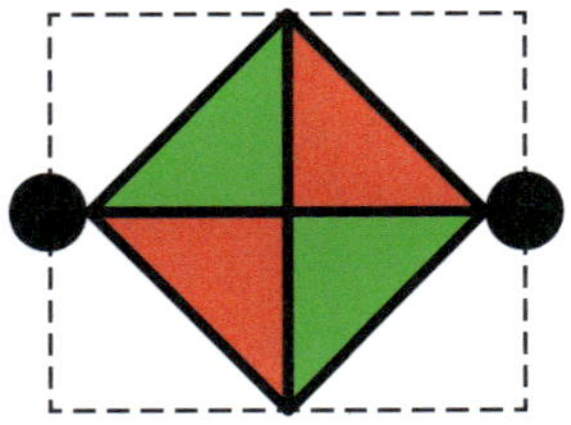

Side Tile

Side Tile

Corner Tiles not shown were Auto Generated by Illustrator

Creating Start and End Tiles

Start and End Tiles are used to give a finished look to an open path.

Start and End Tiles With the Same Height

Pattern Brushes can be formatted with Start Tiles and End Tiles to complete the look of an open path or to create detailed and complex artwork for an illustration.

1) **Design the Side Tile.** Create the repeating part of the design. If it is more than one object, align objects horizontally, draw a Bounding Box around them and group everything together. Drag the group into the Brushes Panel to create a new Pattern Brush.

2) **Design the Start Tile.** This is the Pattern Brush's starting point on an open path. Make the start design the same height as the Side Tile. Add a Bounding Box and group everything together. Hold down the Option Key and drag the group to the Start Tile position in the Brushes Panel *(second to the last tile)*.

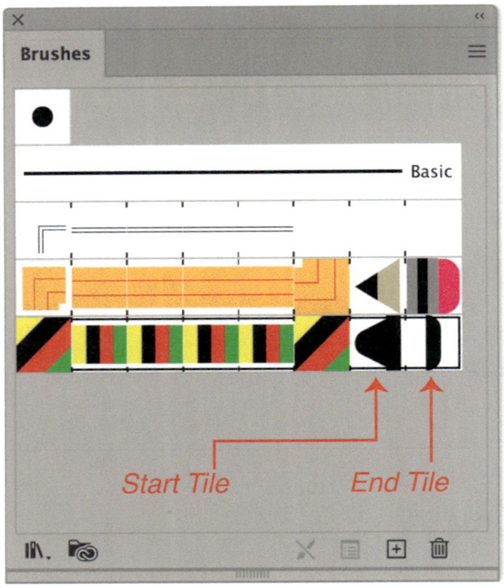

3) **Design the End Tile.** This is the last part of the Pattern Brush's path. Make the End Tile the same height as the Side Tile. Add a Bounding Box and group everything together. Hold down the Option Key and drag the group to the End Tile position in the Brushes Panel *(last tile)*.

4) **Test the Pattern Brush.** Draw an open path and apply the Pattern Brush. If there is space showing between the tiles, adjust the Bounding Boxes and replace the tiles.

The Outside and Inside Corner Tiles for both Pattern Brushes below are Auto Generated options selected in the Brushes Panel.

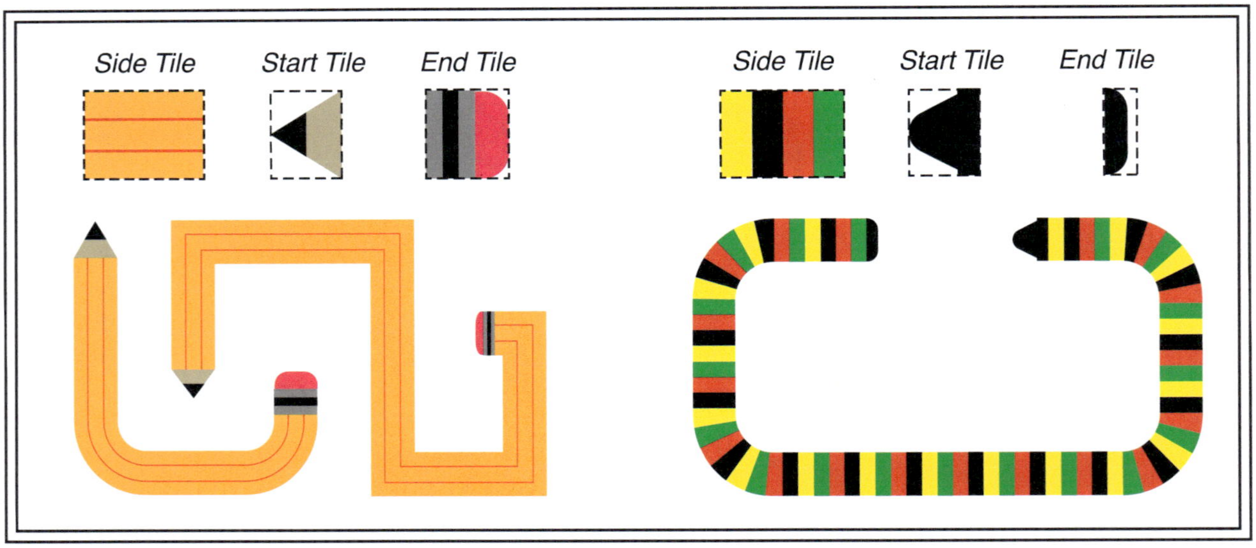

TIP: Precision is the key to making seamless Pattern Brushes and saving time. Use Smart Guides, check measurements and view objects in Outline Mode when designing the various tiles for a Pattern Brush. Enclose each design in a carefully sized Bounding Box.

Start and End Tiles With Different Heights

By default, Pattern Brush tiles are aligned to the center of a path. When the Start, Side and End Tiles are **different heights,** their respective Bounding Boxes must be created in such a way that even though the Bounding Boxes align horizontally on the path, **the designs IN the Bounding Boxes align with each other.** Once the concept is mastered, the possibility of making some fun and crazy Pattern Brushes is oh so close!

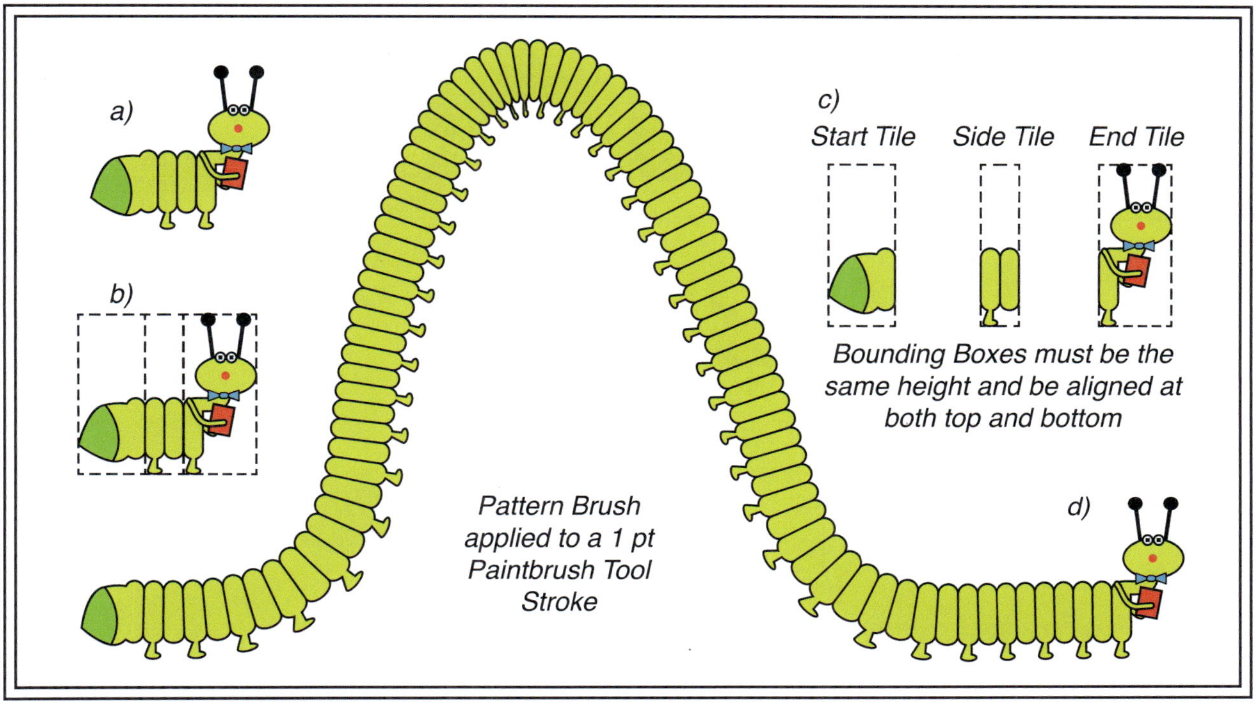

1) **Create the Side Tile, The Start Tile and the End Tile.** The designs should align with each other even if they aren't the same height *(a).*

2) **Draw a Bounding Box around each tile.** Make sure Smart Guides is turned on. Draw Bounding Boxes in Outline View using the Rectangle Tool. The top of each Bounding Box must be as tall as the highest point of any of the designs. The bottom of each Bounding Box must be as low as the lowest point of any of the designs *(b)(c).* Make sure no color is selected for either the Stroke or Fill on the Bounding Boxes. Send the Bounding Boxes to the back.

3) **Make the Pattern Brush.** Follow the instructions on the previous page to create the Pattern Brush. Test the Pattern Brush on an open path to make sure the tiles align properly *(d).* If the Pattern Brush is not seamless, check the alignment of the Bounding Boxes and the designs. Edit as necessary.

TIP: The point at which the path begins when it is drawn is where the Start Tile is placed. If the path is drawn from the left to right side of the artboard, the Start Tile will be on the left side of the path. If the path is drawn from the right to the left side of the artboard, the Start Tile will be on the right and it will be upside down. The path can be flipped right side up using one of the Flip options in the Brushes Panel.

More Start and End Tiles

The Pattern Brushes on this page illustrate more ways Start and End Tiles can be used in a variety of applications. To edit the Pattern Brush after it is applied to a path, select the path and go to Object>Path>Outline Stroke. Press Shift+Command+G to ungroup. Use the Direct Selection Tool *(Keyboard Shortcut A)* to select and change individual anchor points and/or lines.

Challenges With Directional End Tiles

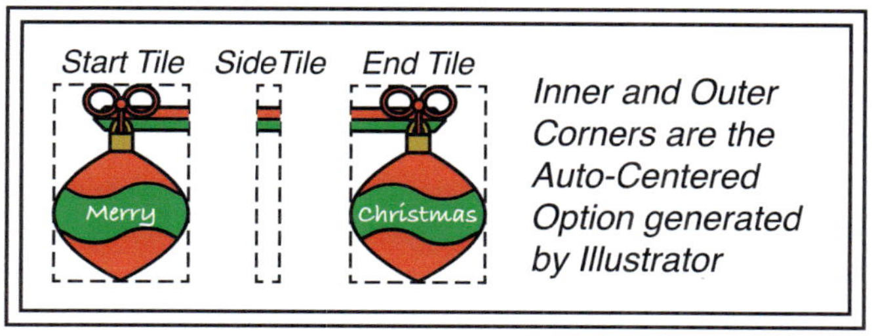

a)

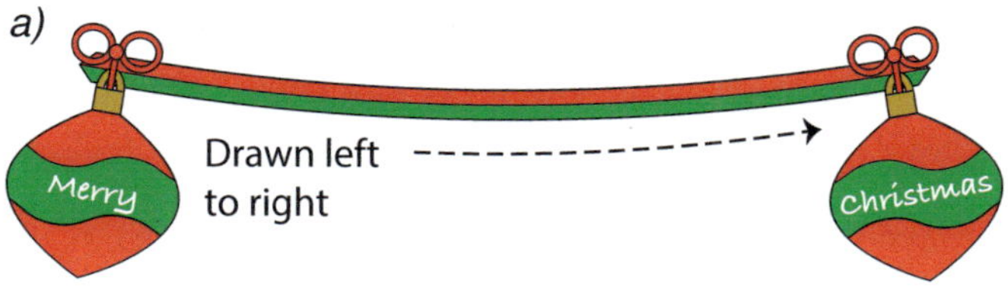

b)

When Start and End Tiles have words that need to appear in a certain direction, it may become necessary to swap them, based on the type of path they are applied to.

This ornament Pattern Brush works perfectly on an open path with "Merry" on the left and "Christmas" on the right as long as the path is drawn from left to right *(a)*. But it does NOT work for the type of path that changes directions *(b)*.

Swapping the Start and End Tiles is the only way to have the words appear in the right order. **Make a second Pattern Brush** with swapped Start and End Tiles when the text doesn't display as desired.

When text is not involved, experiment with drawing the path right to left and try using the Flip Across or Flip Along options in the Brushes Panel.

Colorization of Pattern Brushes

Four Colorization Methods for a Pattern Brush are available in the Pattern Brush Options Dialogue Box. If "None" is selected, the Pattern Brush doesn't change even if the Stroke color of the path it is applied to is changed. When any of the other three methods are checked, the Pattern Brush will change as shown below, if the Stroke color of the path it is applied to is changed. Experiment with the various options to become familiar with how they can change the Pattern Brush.

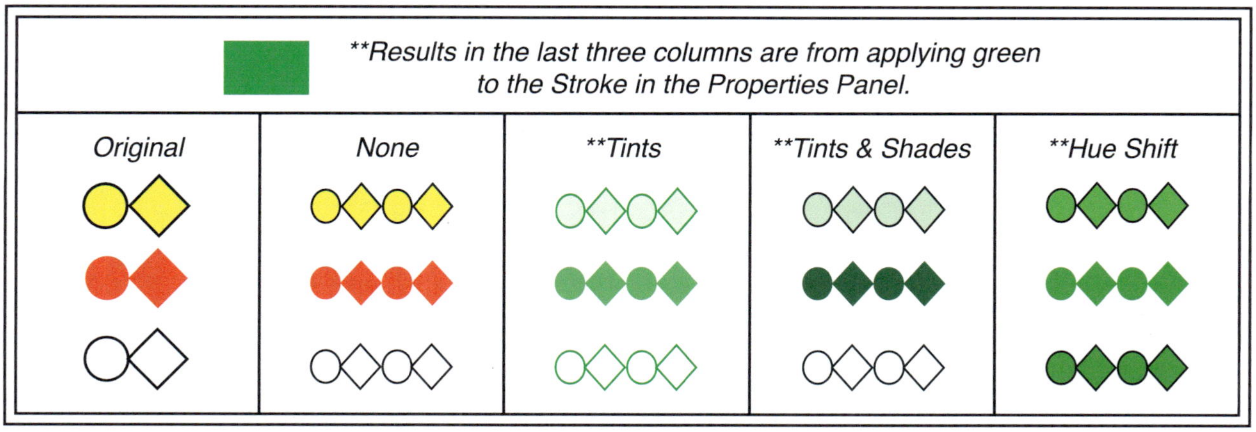

NOTE: *The most reliable way to change the color of a Pattern Brush is to recolor the original artwork and make a new Pattern Brush.*

Pattern Brush Tiles

(used in Pattern Brushes on the following page)

Outer Corner Tile

Side Tile (on the heart)

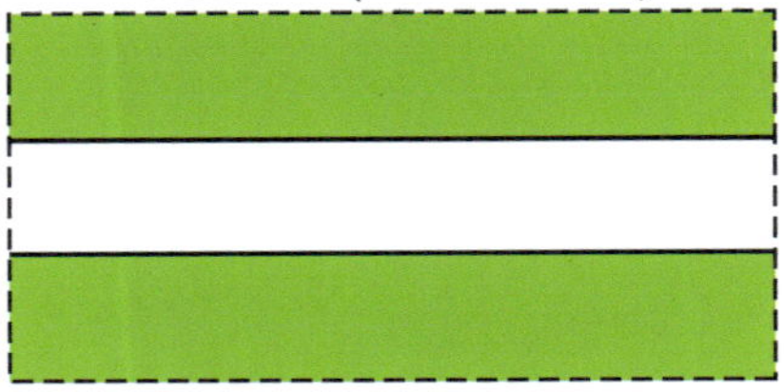

Inner Corner Tile

Outer Corner Tile

Side Tile

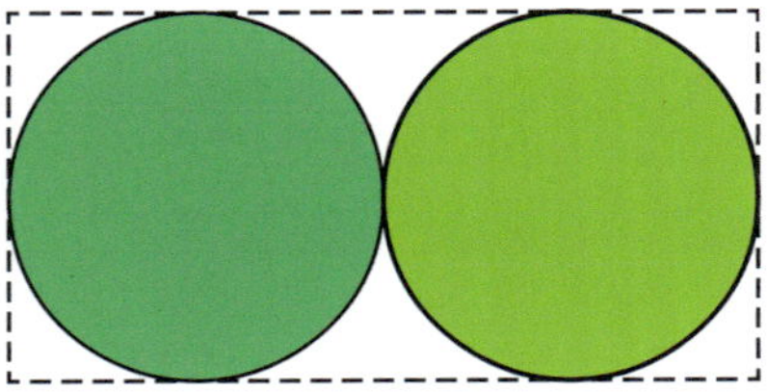

Outer Corner Tile

Side Tile

Side Tile

Spacing, Fitting and Flipping

Learn how to edit a Pattern Brush for different sizes, shapes and purposes.

Resizing a Pattern Brush

Pattern Brushes can be resized in three different ways:

1) **Change the Stroke value in the Properties Panel.** A larger Stroke number will increase the size of the Pattern Brush while a smaller Stroke number will decrease it. Even a slight increase or decrease can bring design changes. Stroke sizes can be typed in manually to increase or decrease by fractions of a point. Sometimes changing the Stroke size can cause distortion of the Pattern Brush, especially if the paths are curved or the angle of the corner is less than 90°.

2) **Change the Scale in the Pattern Brush Options Dialogue Box.** With the Scale set to "Fixed", increase or decrease the Scale percentage rate to increase or decrease the size of the Pattern Brush. The other options will be grayed out unless an electronic drawing device is being used.

3) **Resize the Original Artwork.** If the Pattern Brush is too large with a .25 pt Stroke, resize the original artwork to reduce its size. Either make a new Pattern Brush or edit the original one. Make sure all objects are grouped together, then go to Object>Transform>Scale and enter a value under 100%. To prevent distortion when resizing an object or group of objects, make sure Uniform and Scale Corners and Scale Strokes and Effects are all checked. After resizing each of the tile designs, hold down the Option Key and drag the tiles one by one into their proper location in the Brushes Panel *(see page 34)*. When the Pattern Brush Options Dialogue Box pops up, click OK.

TIP: If a Stroke is too thin after reducing the artwork, increase the weight of the Stroke in the Properties Panel BEFORE dragging it into the Brushes Panel.

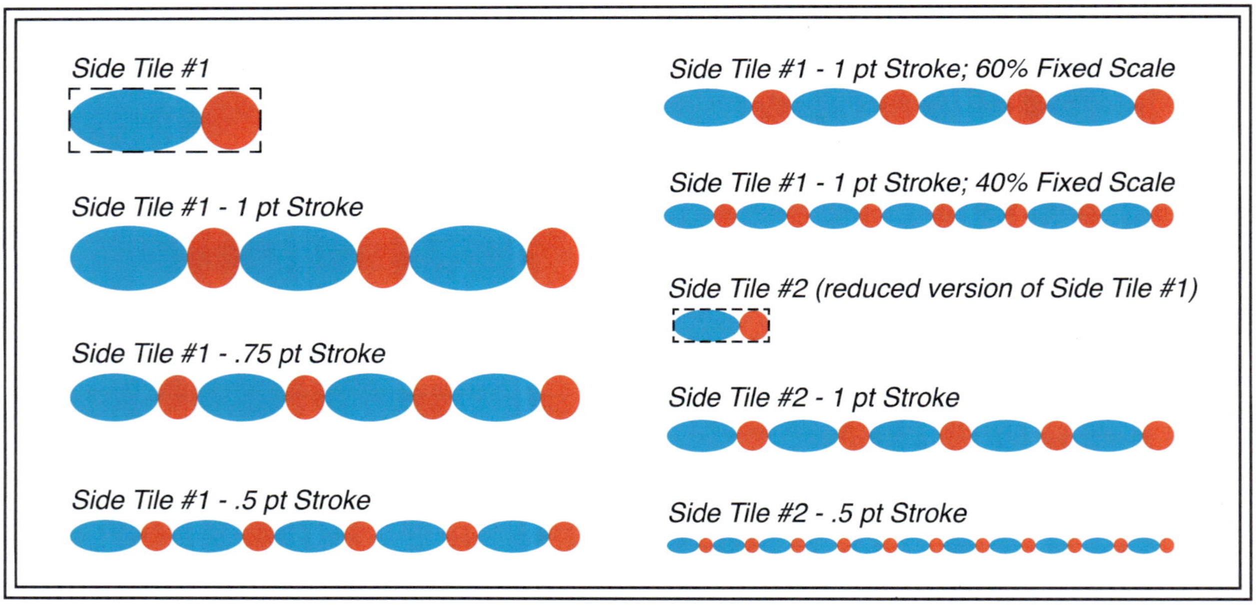

The more complex a Pattern Brush becomes, the more challenging it can be to design it with precision. Start by creating larger-than-needed elements for a Pattern Brush so every tiny detail can be examined for accuracy. When the artwork is complete, group it together, make a Pattern Brush and test it to make sure there are no hidden problems. Make a copy of the original design, then resize the artwork to the desired size for the Pattern Brush.

Fit Options

The Pattern Brush Options Dialogue Box offers three choices for fitting a Pattern Brush on a Path. In the examples below, even though **the squares are exactly the same size,** they look significantly different based on the Fit Option selected in the Pattern Brush Options Dialogue Box. With simpler Pattern Brushes, the differences may be less noticeable.

Stretch to Fit Option - This is the default option. When Stretch to Fit is selected, Illustrator may either shorten or lengthen the Side Tile to perfectly fit a path. In some instances, this causes the pattern to look uneven or skewed. If this happens, experiment with one of the other fit options.

Add Space to Fit Option - Based upon the length of a path, when this option is selected, Illustrator evenly adds space between the Side Tiles so the Pattern Brush is evenly distributed. In the example below, the Pattern Brush looks incomplete.

Approximate Path Option - When this option is selected, Illustrator may move the pattern to the inside or outside of the path so the Pattern Tiles fit and remain evenly spaced.

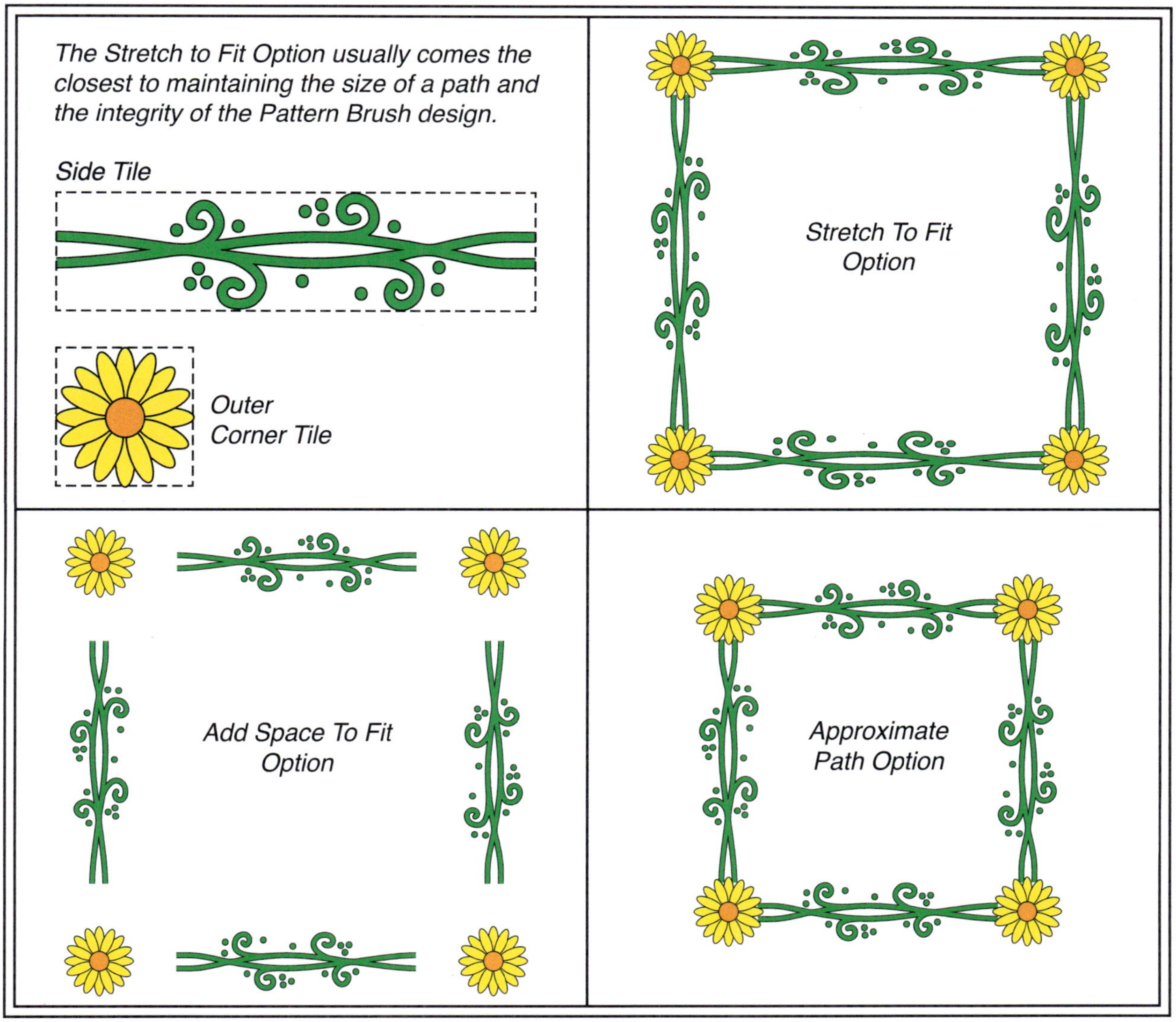

Spacing Options For Pattern Brushes

Customize the appearance of a Pattern Brush by adjusting the spacing of its objects. The simplest and fastest way for adjusting single objects, discussed on Page 19, is to **select a percentage value for spacing in the Pattern Brush Options Dialogue Box**. It is not an exact science and may require several attempts of adjusting the percentage to get the desired spacing.

When multiple objects are in a Side Tile, **build the spacing into the object group itself with a Bounding Box**, prior to dragging it into the Brushes Panel.

1) **Create objects** and align them horizontally *(a)*.

2) **Adjust spacing to the desired width.** Select each of the objects and use arrow keys to nudge them into place *(b)*. Group the objects together.

3) **Create a Bounding Box** with the rectangle tool that fits around the top and bottom of the objects. Add space on the sides as desired. Remove the Stroke and Fill color from the Bounding Box. Move it to the back and group everything together *(c)*.

4) **Create a Pattern Brush.** Drag the group into the Brushes Panel. Test the Pattern Brush by applying it to a path. Adjust the width of the bounding box if the spacing is too wide or too narrow.

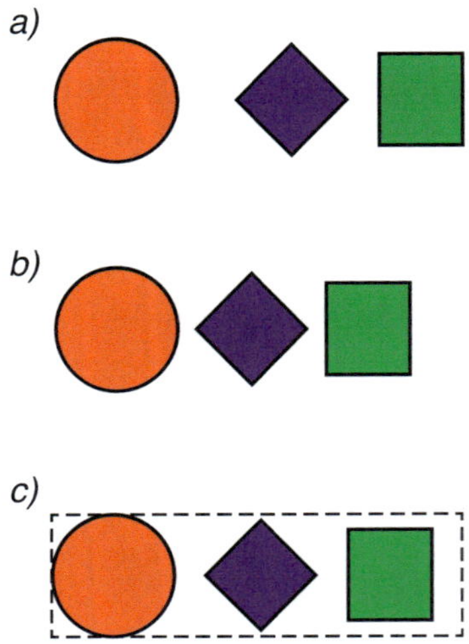

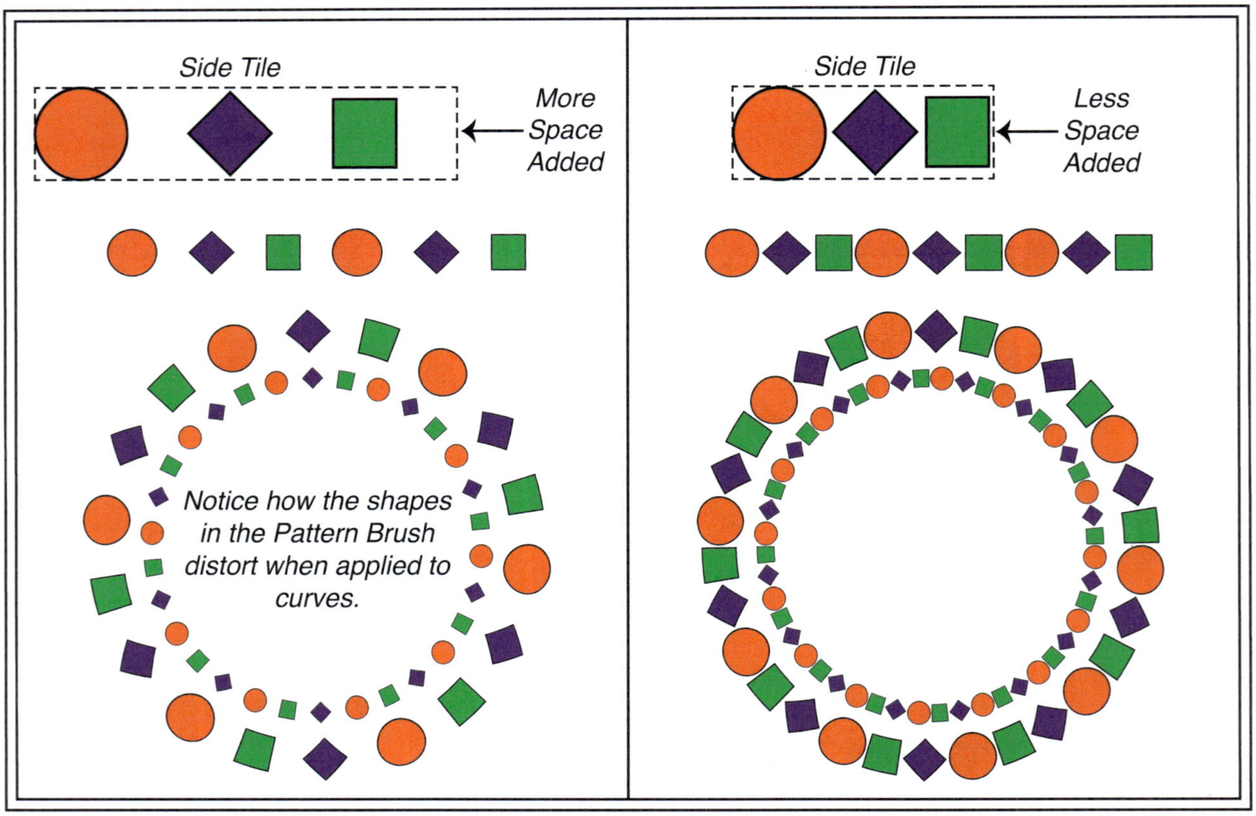

Negative Spacing For Pattern Brushes

Overlapping a Pattern Brush's Side Tile can result in intricate and beautiful results. Achieve the overlap through formatting the Side Tile for negative spacing in its Bounding Box. In order to fully appreciate the resulting design, <u>any Fill color used in an object should have a reduced opacity</u>.

1) **Create an object with either a Stroke only, a transparent Fill only or a Stroke and transparent Fill**. To change the opacity of the Fill of an object without affecting its Stroke, select the object and go to Window>Appearance. In the Appearance Panel, select a Fill color, then click on Opacity (under the Fill color) and type in a value under 50%. Exit out of the Appearance Panel by clicking on the X in the top left corner.

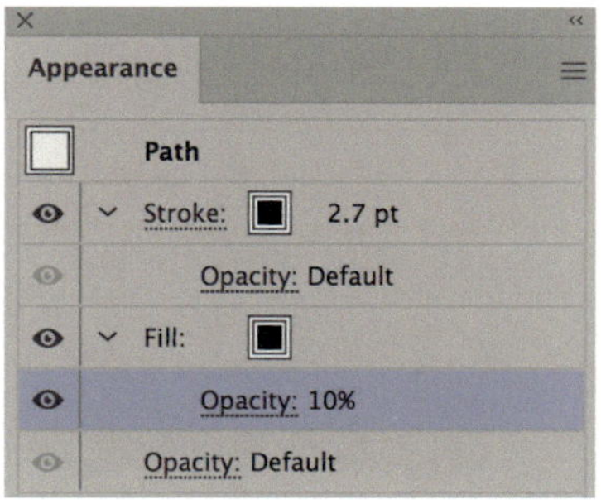

2) **Make a Bounding Box** that is the same height as the object. The width of the Bounding Box should be narrower than the object. The design in the Side Tile will overlap based on the width of the Bounding Box. Remember to remove any Stroke color on the Bounding Box and send it to the back. Align the object and Bounding Box to center, group them and drag them into the Brushes Panel to create a new Pattern Brush.

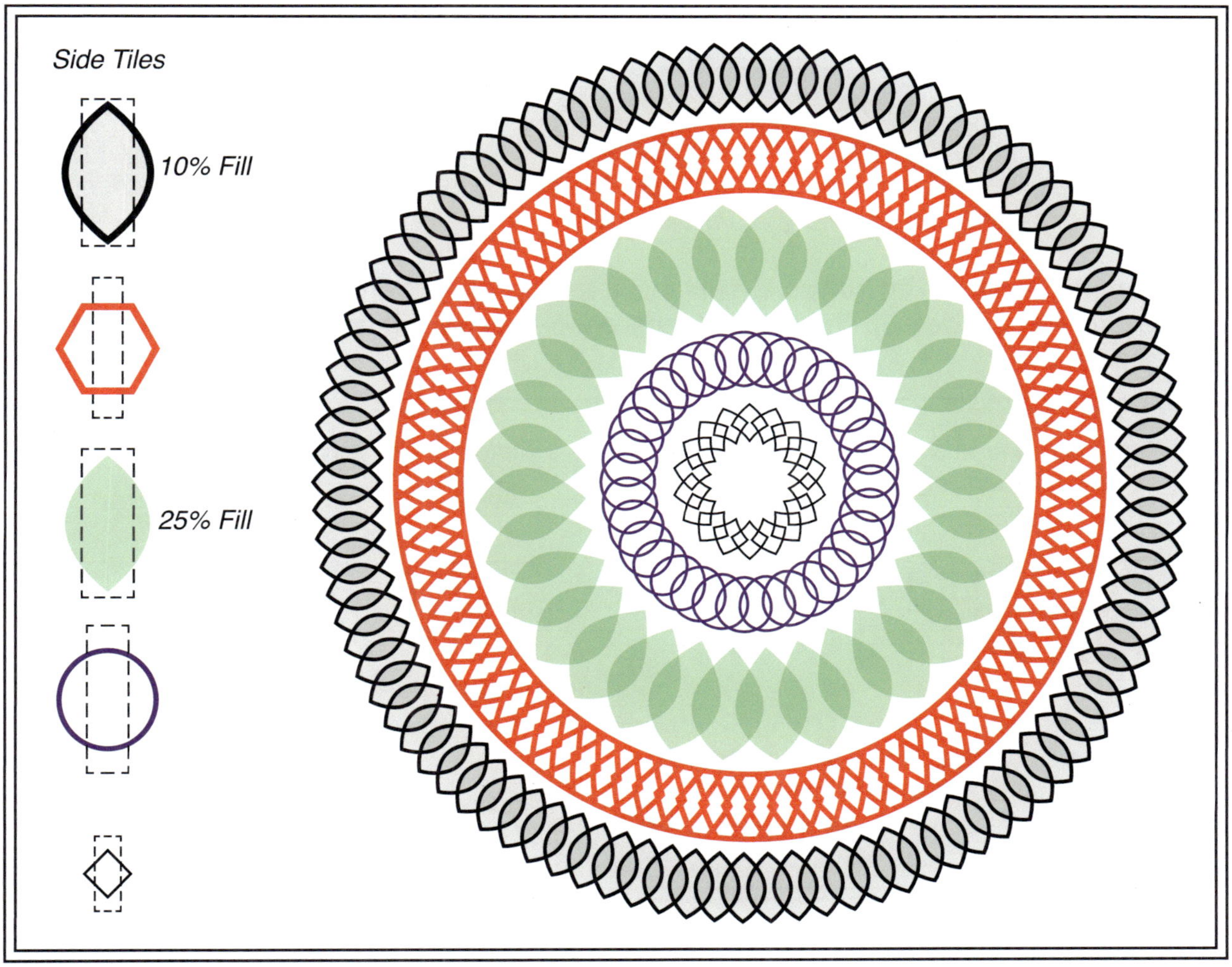

Flip Across and Flip Along

Flip Across is an option **in the Pattern Brush Options Dialogue Box.** Flip Across offers directional flexibility for a Pattern Brush, reflecting the Pattern Brush's Side Tile horizontally along a path *(red line below)*. This option can be turned on and off.

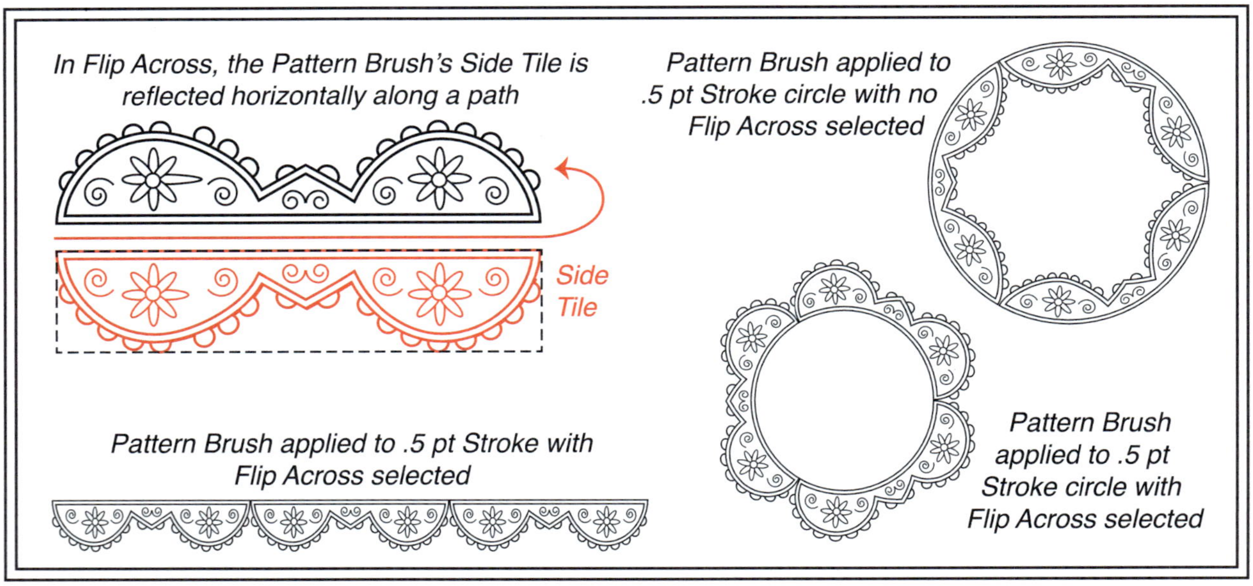

TIP: The direction of a Pattern Brush can be flipped when a path is created. Drag a rectangle tool from top right to bottom left to "flip across" the Pattern Brush. Draw a path from right to left to "flip across AND along" the Pattern Brush. Look for other "on the fly" ways to change a Pattern Brush's direction when objects are created!

Flip Along is similar to Flip Across, except that it reflects the Pattern Brush's Side Tile vertically along a path *(red line below)*. This option is most easily observed when artwork has a distinct right and left side.

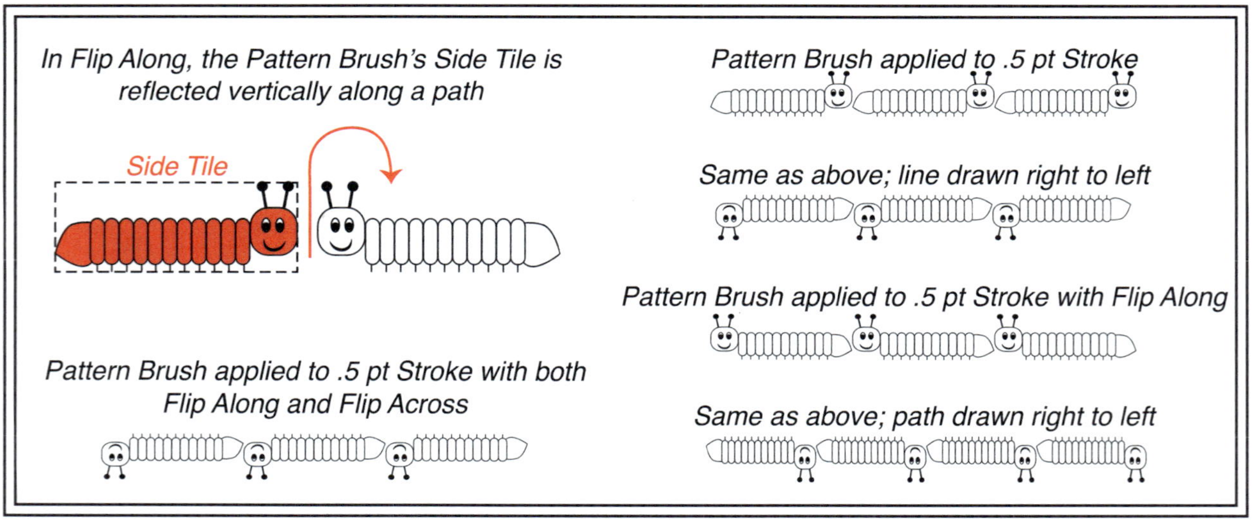

NOTE: Both Flip Across and Flip Along can be selected at the same time.

Editing Shortcut

Any option in a Pattern Brush can be changed. Double click on the Pattern Brush in the Brushes Panel and the Pattern Brush Dialogue Box opens, giving access to all the options. When changes are made and OK is clicked, another Dialogue Box opens, asking whether or not to apply the changes to any existing Strokes. If multiple paths using the same Pattern Brush are in the active document, checking "Apply to Strokes" changes all the paths. If "Leave Strokes" is selected, none of the paths will be changed. To change the path manually, select it and click on the Pattern Brush in the Brushes Panel. The most recent changes will now be reflected on that path.

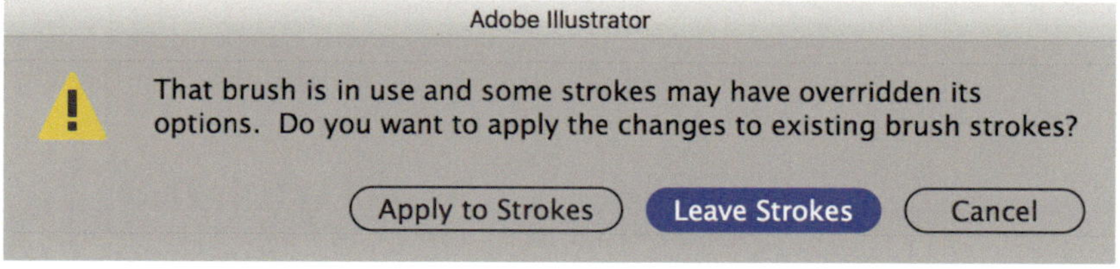

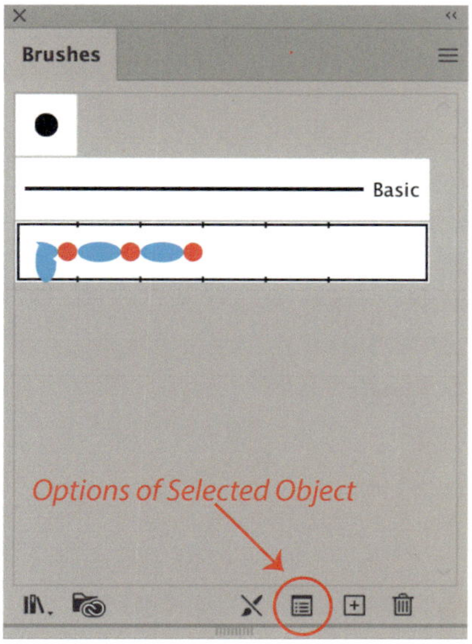

There is a shortcut. Select the Pattern Brush path to be changed and click on the Options of Selected Object icon at the bottom Tool Bar of the Brushes Panel. *(The icon is grayed out if a path isn't selected).* This brings up the Stroke Options *(Pattern Brush)* Dialogue Box. Any changes will be made immediately, but **only in the Pattern Brush on the selected path.** No Dialogue Box asking if changes are to be made on all paths appears. Make sure Preview is checked to see the changes applied. Click OK to accept changes. The few seconds it saves can add up over time, especially when multiple edits are needed to tweak the Pattern Brush.

TIP: In some cases, there may be a need to use both Flip Along and Flip Across options in a single illustration. Become familiar with how each of the options affects a Pattern Brush.

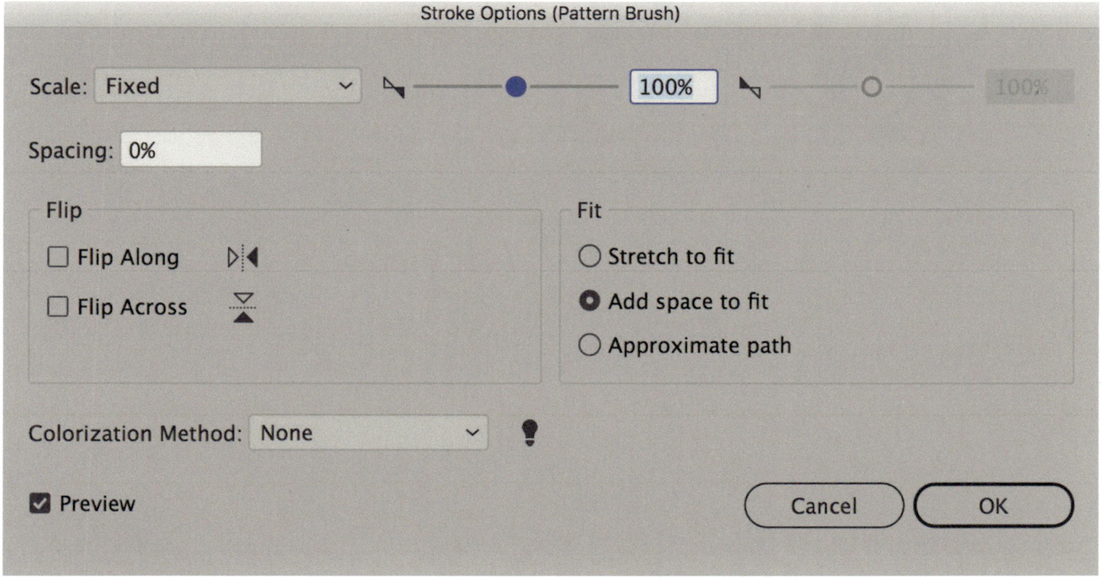

Pattern Brush Tiles

These are the tiles used in the Pattern Brushes on following page

Side Tile

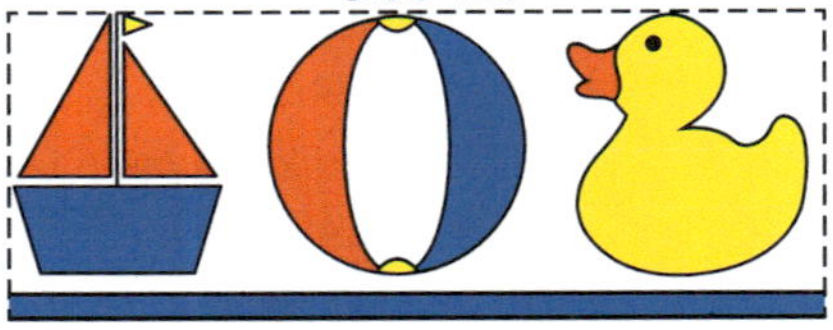

Outer Corner Tile

Side Tile

Outer Corner Tile

Side Tile

Ways To Use Pattern Brushes

This section contain examples of things to do and ways to use Pattern Brushes. While this is by no means an exhaustive list, it will hopefully inspire many new and useful creative ideas!

A zipper can be added to an article of clothing in an illustration, adding another level of interest and texture. The Auto-Between Option in the Auto Generated Tiles can be used for square corners, but this is one Pattern Brush that works best with curves or straight lines. Once created, the zipper can be recolored, resized and reused over and over again.

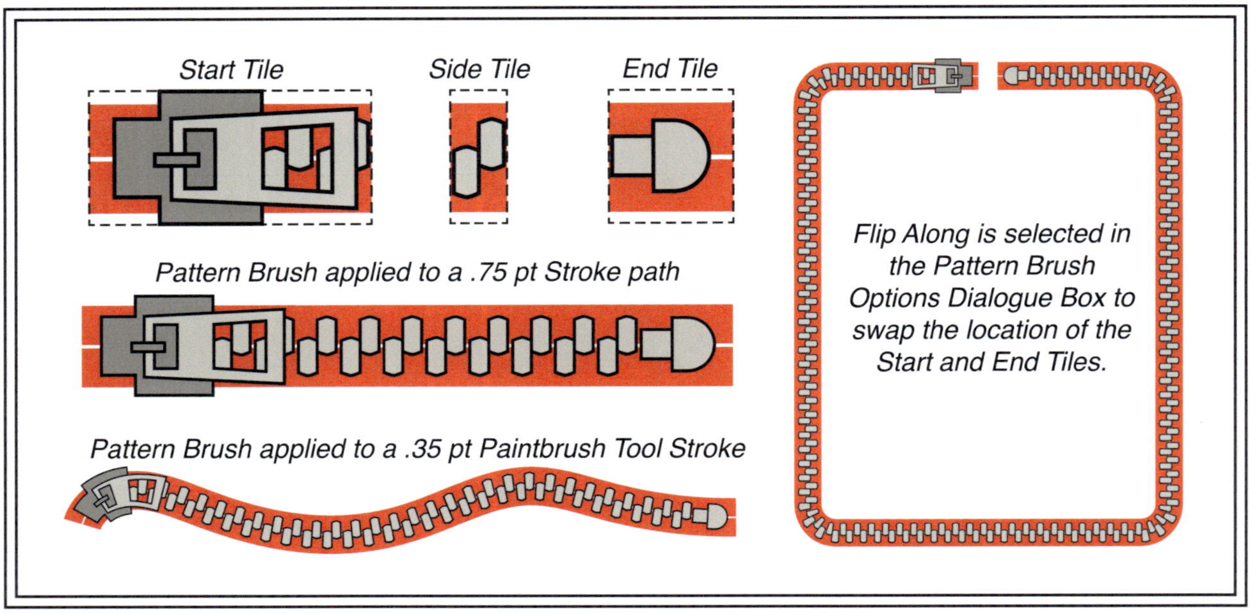

Fencing can be placed into a Pattern Brush and used in illustrations. Leave the picket off the right side and make an End Tile with one stand-alone picket. The size and color can be adjusted for different projects. This Pattern Brush is best suited for a path without corners, but when a corner is needed, try the Auto-Centered Option from the Auto Generated Corner Tiles.

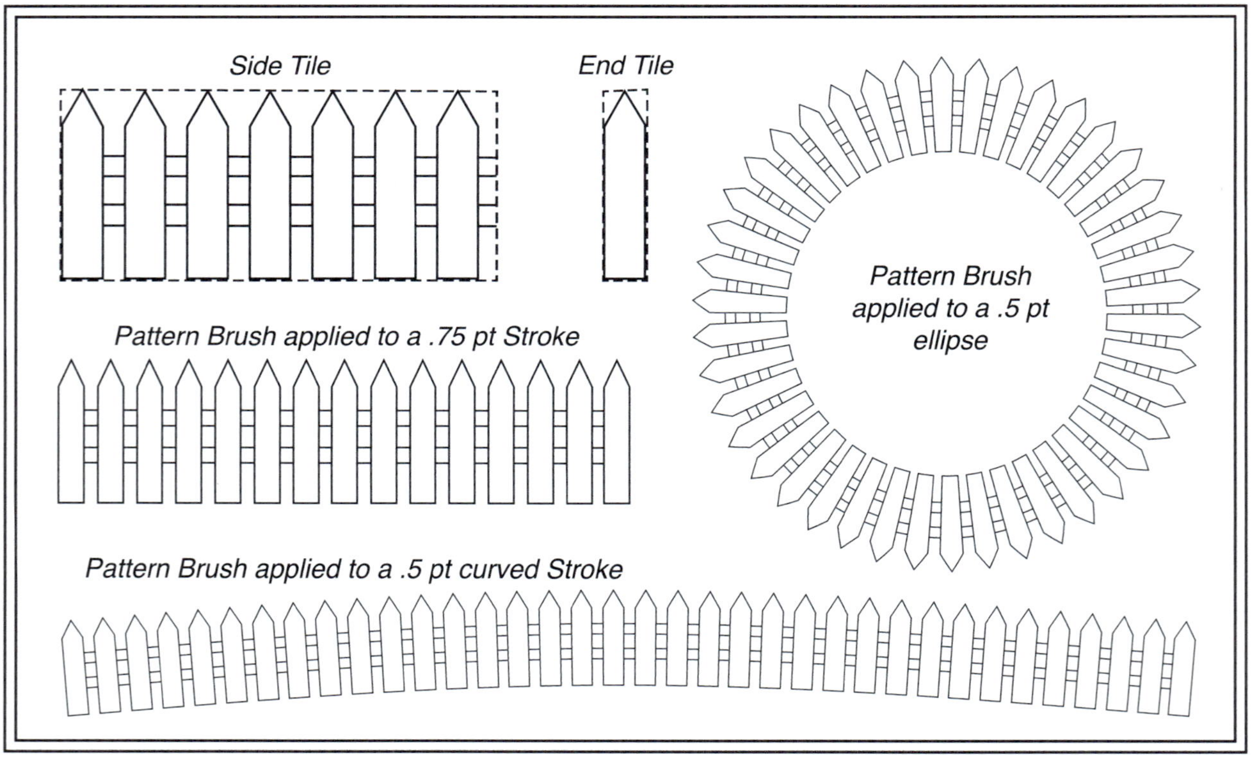

Pennant banners make a cute addition to the background of an illustration for a children's book. Create one flag for each color.

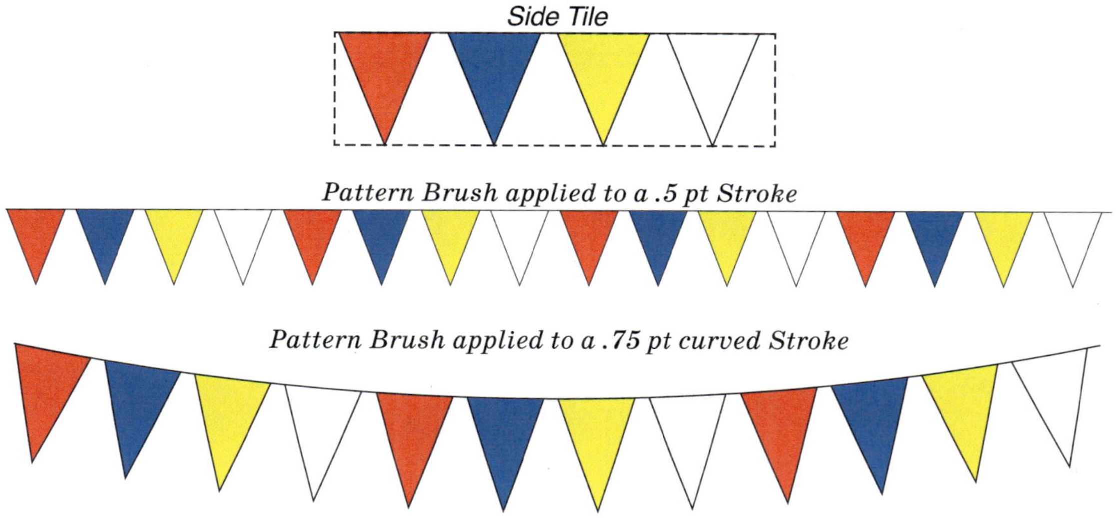

Stitched seams on a Pattern Brush allow the addition of detail to a pair of jeans. Directions for making a stitched Pattern Brush:

1) Draw a .25" x 2" rectangle without a Stroke. Select the Fill color of the fabric.
2) Draw two 2" wide 1 pt black strokes. Align them and place on top and bottom of the rectangle.
3) Add a 2" wide 2 pt Stroke with a Stroke color for stitching. Align it to the horizontal center of the rectangle.
4) Select the center Stroke. Go to the Stroke Tool *(access by clicking on the word Stroke in the Properties Panel).* Check Dashed Line and type 7 in the first box and 4 in the second box. For longer stitches, increase the number in the first box. For stretching the stitches further apart, increase the number in the second box.
5) Select all strokes and go to Object>Path>Outline Stroke. Dashes become objects and can be ungrouped and manipulated. Tweak the dashes so that when the pattern repeats, the stitches appear seamless.
6) Add Bounding Boxes, group all and make the Pattern Brush.

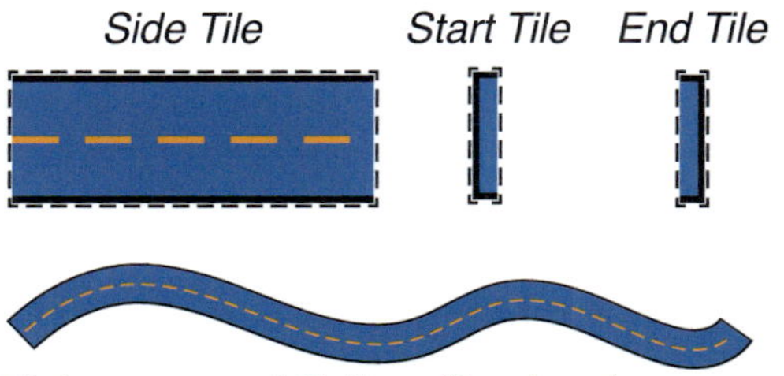

Make a second Pattern Brush using the same Side Tile, but add a Start and End Tile. In some instances, i.e. the stitching at the center line of the jeans, end tiles are needed.

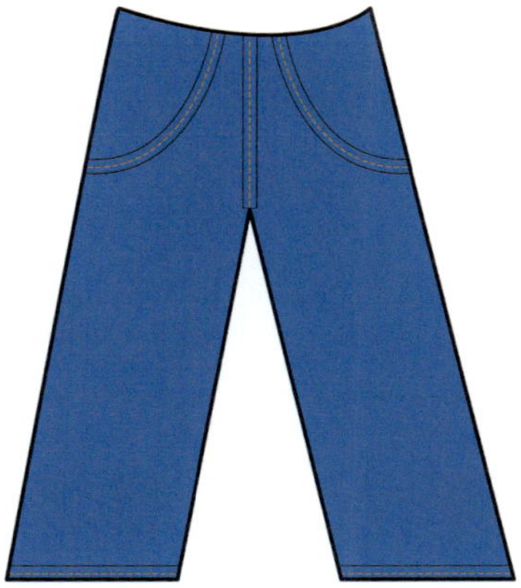

If the Pattern Brush Strokes overlap the outline Stroke of the jeans, 1) tweak the width of the line to make it fit better, or 2) copy the jeans layer without a Fill and paste it on top of other layers. Result is a clean black Stroke over all.

Beaded Jewelry is a fun detail to add to an illustration. Creating all the various pieces from scratch can be tedious. See how easy and quick it can be with a Pattern Brush! Draw a line with the Paintbrush Tool and click on the Pattern Brush. Resize the Stroke value in the Properties Panel to achieve the desired results.

Pipes and Pipe Fittings are repetitious but time-consuming to make if every jog and turn has to be custom drawn. Make a Pattern Brush and the task becomes easier for this job and any others like it in the future. The challenging part of designing this Pattern Brush is figuring out how to correctly place the Inner Corner Tile in a Bounding Box to fit with the rest of the tiles. Persistence will pay off! For added detail, change the Fill color to brass and add rivets.

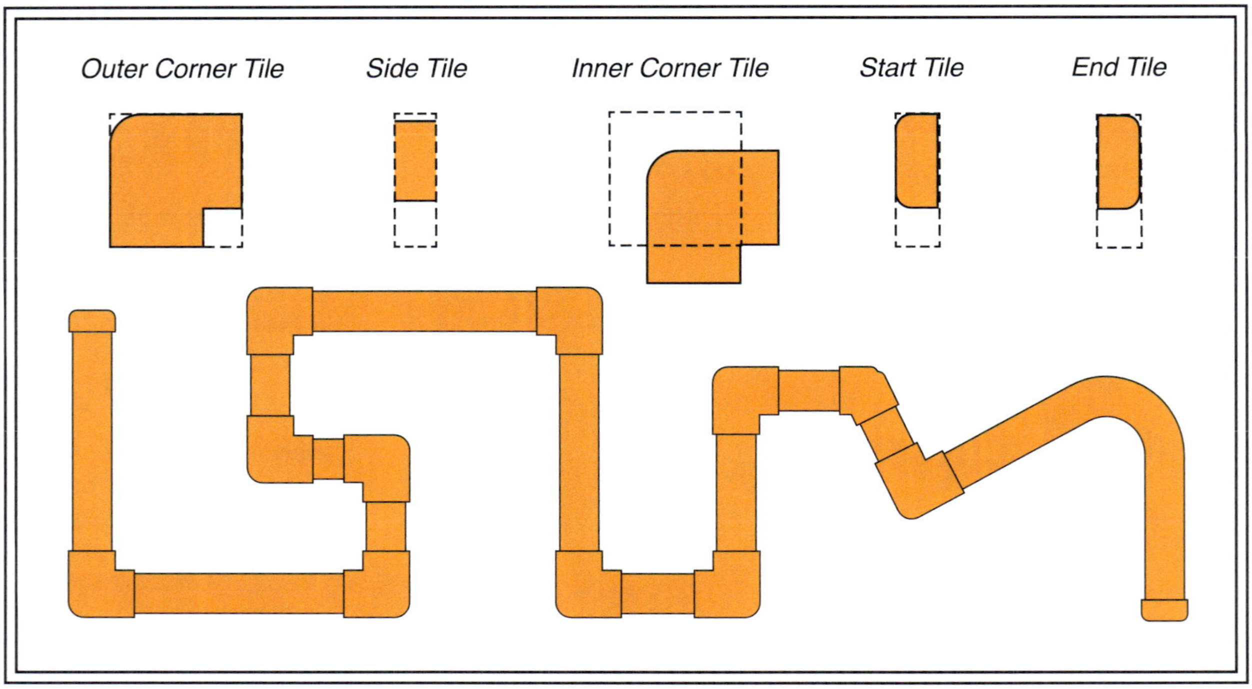

Dashed Strokes open up even more possibilities for interesting and artistic results. Create a design with a color Fill but no Stroke and make a Pattern Brush. Apply the Pattern Brush to a Dashed Stroke. Different dash and gap values change the results. Simple designs work best, but try ANYTHING!

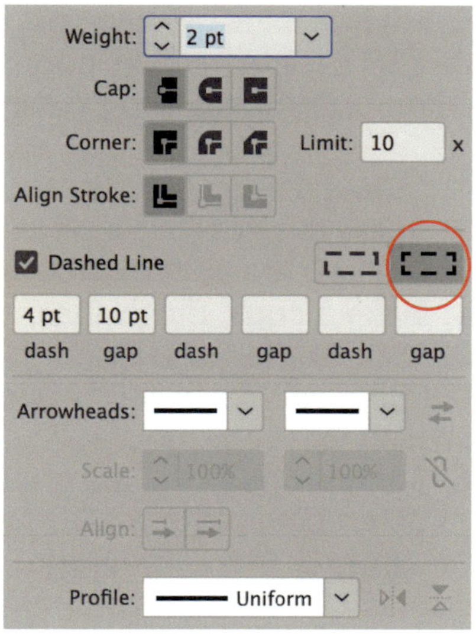

TIP: In the Dashed Line options, select the dashed rectangle on the RIGHT so the design will be evenly centered!

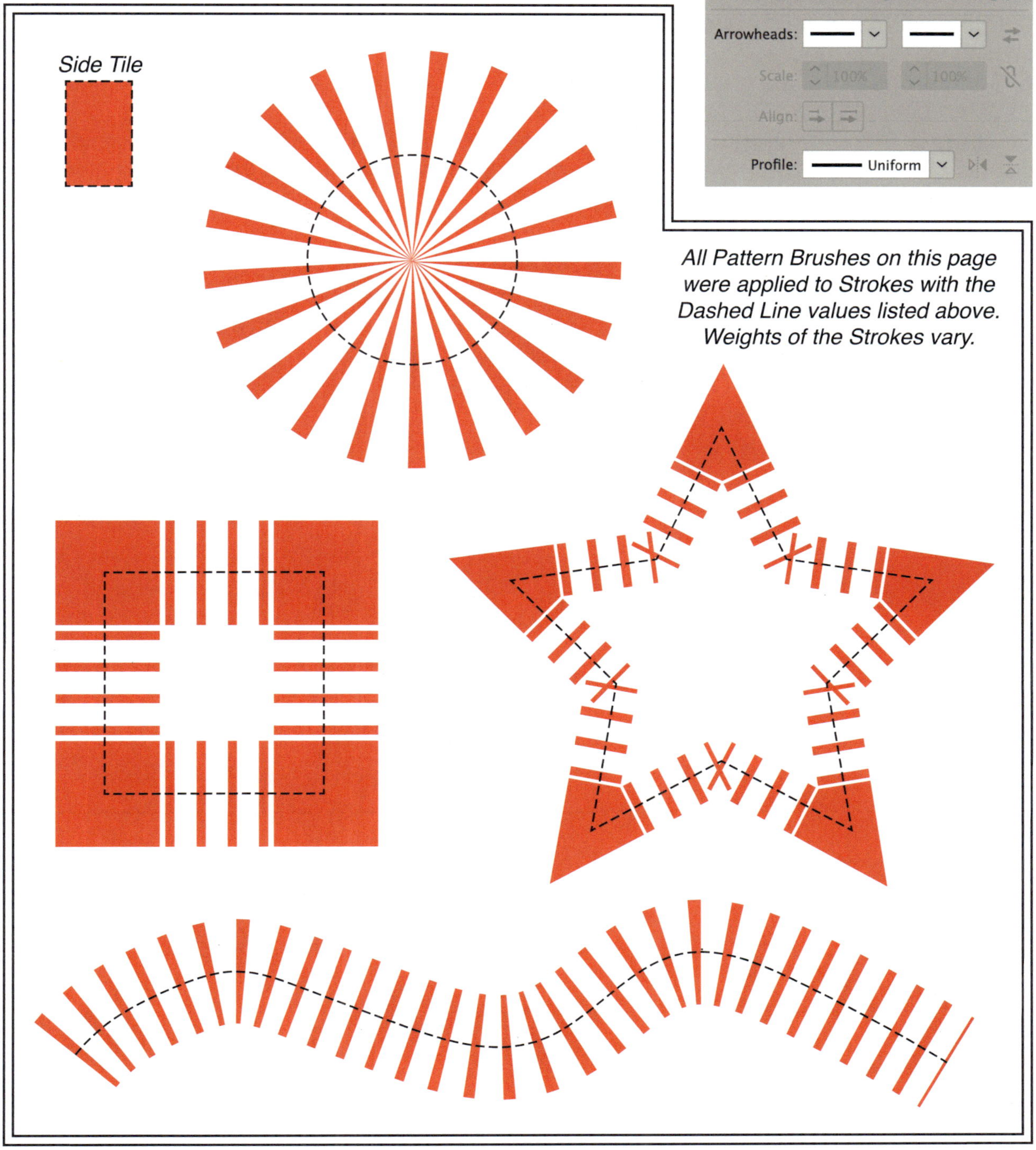

All Pattern Brushes on this page were applied to Strokes with the Dashed Line values listed above. Weights of the Strokes vary.

Gradients must be rasterized before they can be placed in a Pattern Brush. Add a gradient effect AFTER a Pattern Brush is applied to a path and it will NOT have to be rasterized. Experiment with different Gradients and Opacity Settings for different results.

1) **Create** a simple Pattern Brush *(a)*.
2) **Apply** the Pattern Brush to a path *(b)*.
3) **Change the path to an Outline Stroke.** Select path and go to Object>Path>Outline Stroke.
4) **Make a copy.** Select the object, press Command+C and then Command+F to paste it on top.
5) **Apply a gradient**. Select the top layer. Double click the Gradient Tool in the left Toolbar. When the Gradient Dialogue Box opens up, select a gradient. In this example, the Linear Gradient was chosen *(c)*.
6) **Set the Opacity** of the gradient layer to 75%
7) Select both paths but DO NOT GROUP THEM.
8) **Apply a Blending Mode.** With both objects selected, click on Opacity in the Appearance section of the Properties Pane. A drop-down menu will open. Click on the Blending Mode *(by default it is set to Normal)* and select Multiply *(d)*.

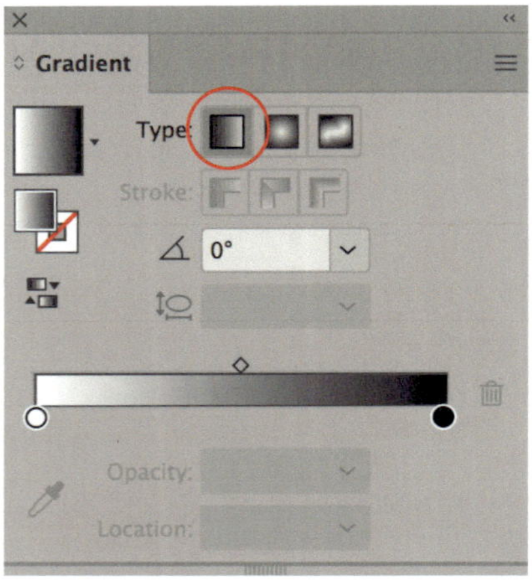

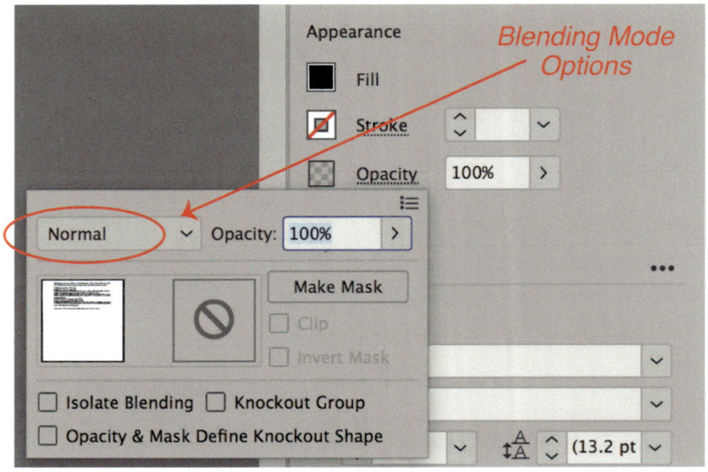

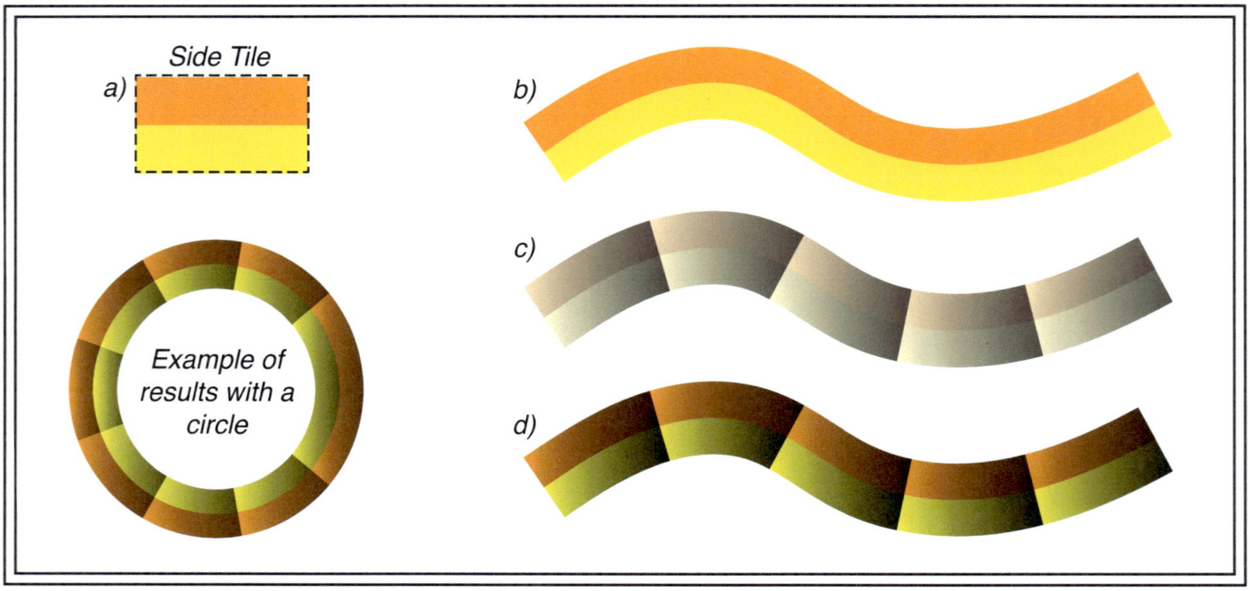

Coloring Pages can be created with strategically placed Strokes and a few Pattern Brushes. Designs can be created for all ages. Side Tiles shown were used in the Pattern Brushes on the Coloring Page below. For best results, use a black Stroke and a white Fill.

Maps and children's book illustrations have repeating objects that can be created with Pattern Brushes and used over and over again.

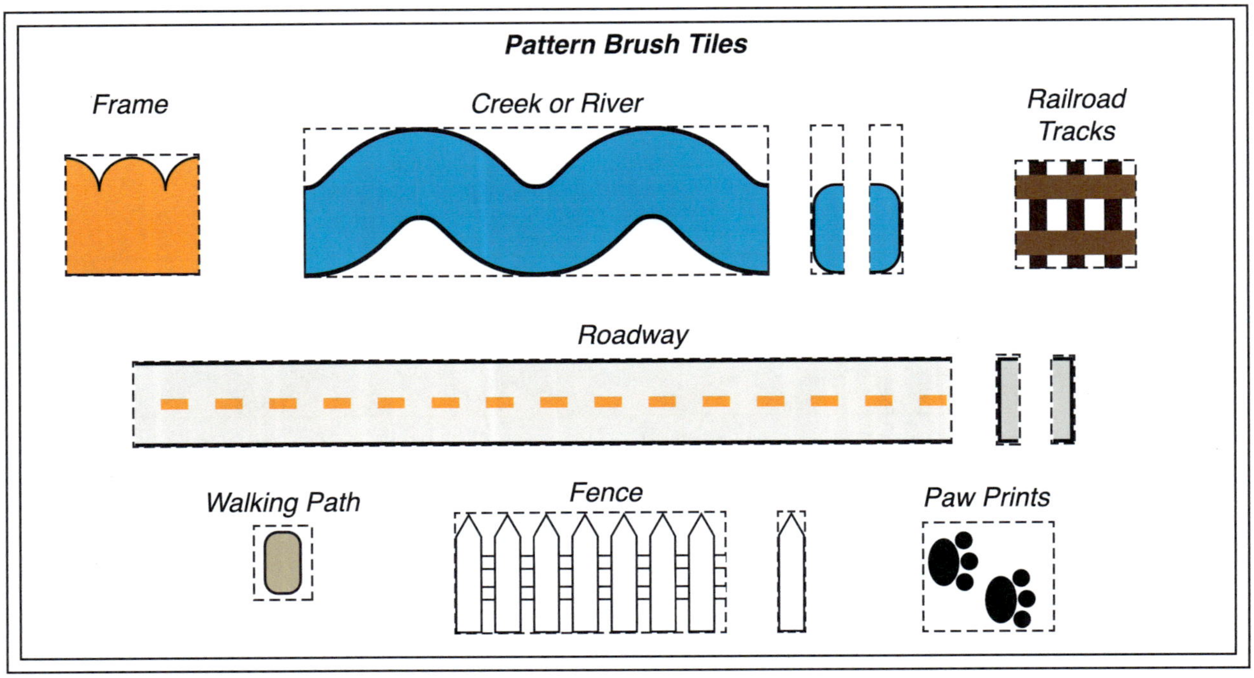

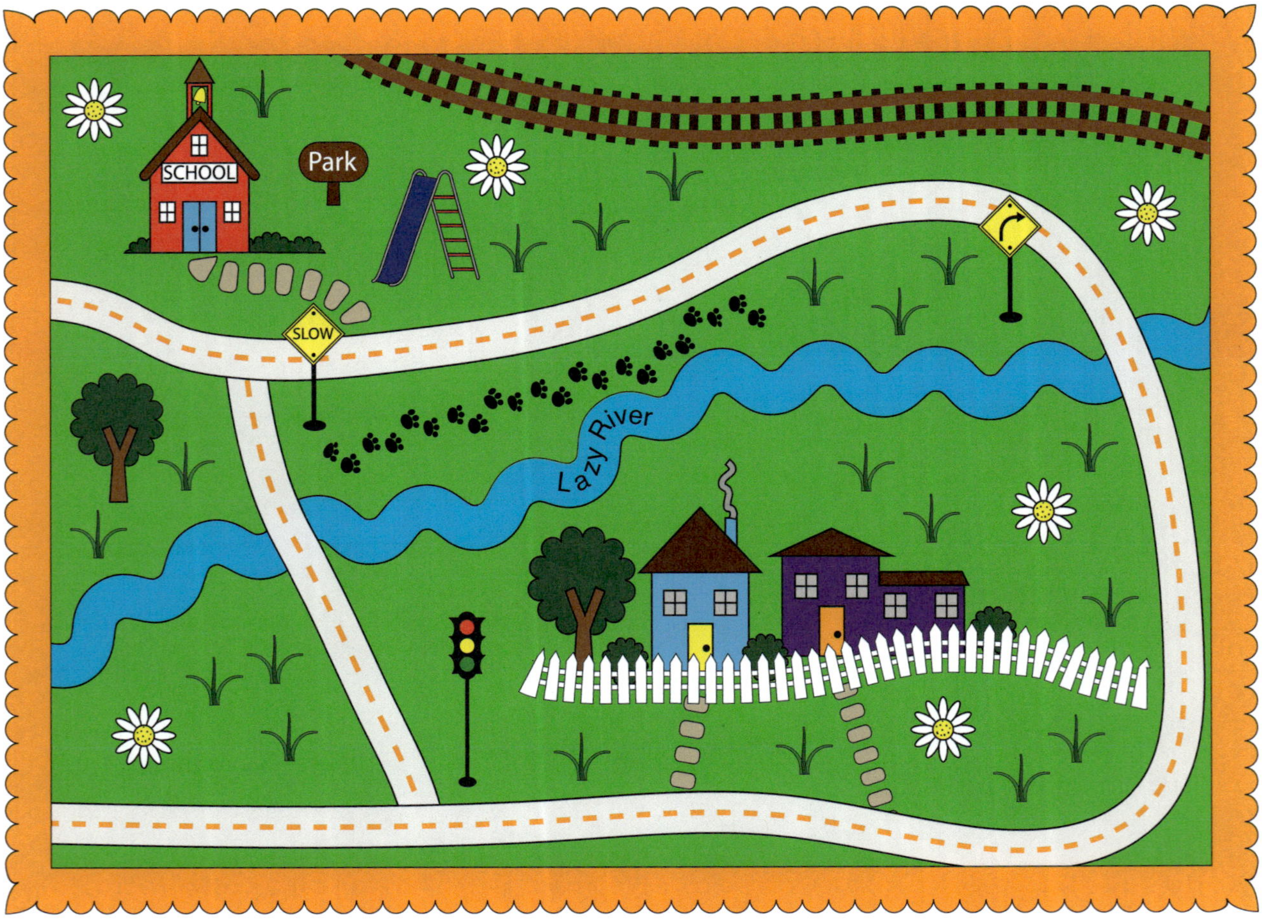

Borders that are created with Pattern Brushes can be used to customize stationery, invitations and cards. They can also be applied to a path and exported as a .pdf or .jpg file to embelish a graphic design in another software program.

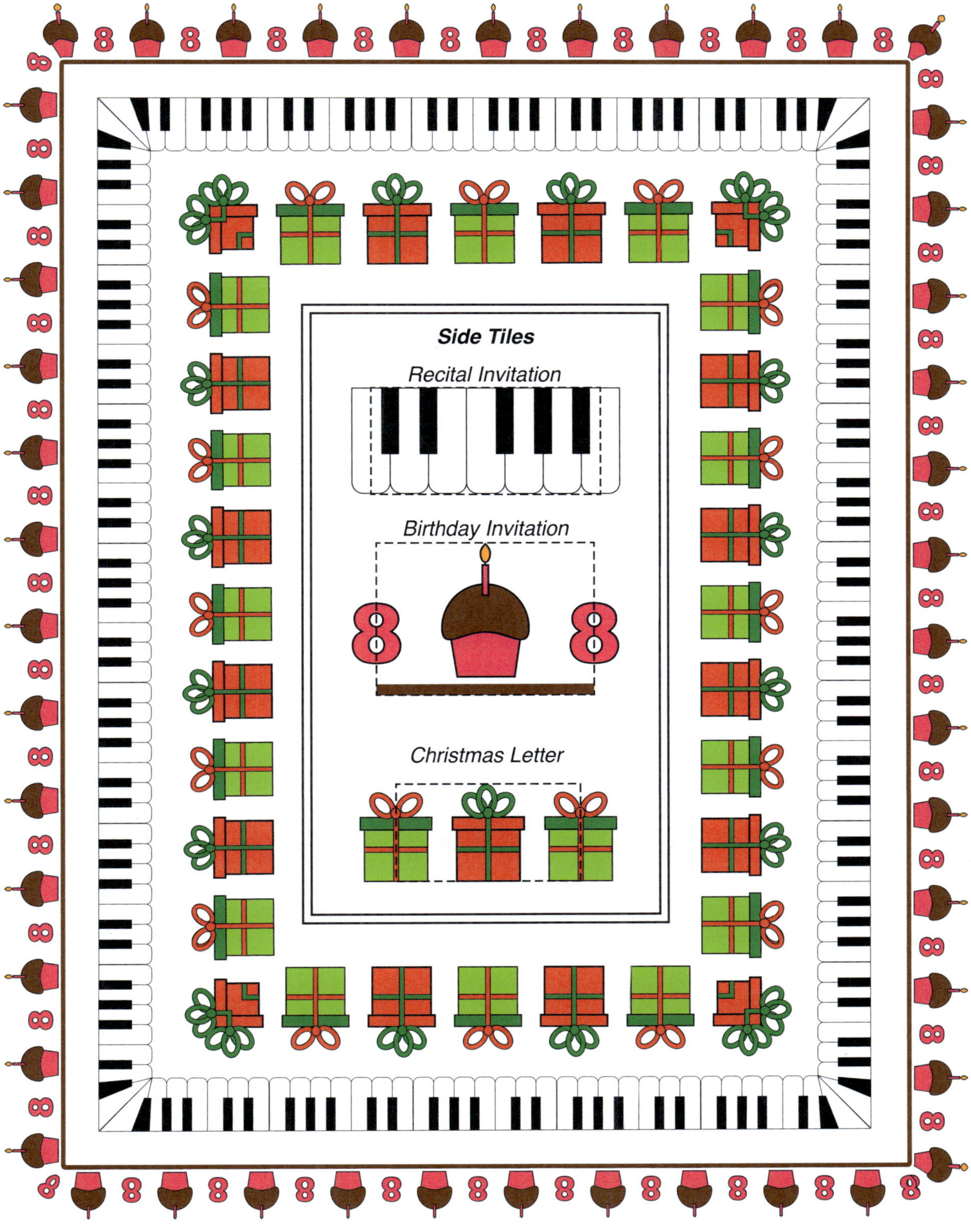

Pattern Brush Tiles

(used in Pattern Brushes on the following page)

Outer Corner Tile

Side Tile

Side Tile

Inner Corner Tile

Side Tile

End Tile

Saving Pattern Brushes and Troubleshooting

Learn how and where to save Pattern Brushes and what do to if problems arise when creating a Pattern Brush.

Saving Brushes

A Pattern Brush will remain in the document it is created in, but it is not automatically available in any other documents. Pattern Brushes can be saved in two different ways.

First, remove any unwanted brushes by selecting them and then clicking on the trashcan located in the lower right corner of the Brushes Panel. The only brushes that cannot be deleted are the Touch Calligraphic Brush and the Basic Brush.

1) **Saving brushes to a Brush Library.** In the Brushes panel, click on <u>either</u> the Brush Libraries Menu Icon in the lower left corner OR the contextual drop-down menu in the top right corner. In either case, a drop-down menu appears. Choose Save Brushes, which brings up a Dialogue Box. Type in a descriptive name for the library and click Save. All active brushes in the Brushes Panel will be saved into a new Brush Library.

<u>You can NOT edit or add to a brush library once it is created.</u>

Opening a saved Brush Library. Click on the Brush Libraries Menu Icon. When the drop-down menu appears, click on User Defined. All added Brush Libraries will be listed in a drop-down menu. Select a library to open it. Any Pattern Brush you use from the library will be added to the current Brushes Panel of the document.

2) **Save Pattern Brushes into a dedicated Pattern Brush document.** Create a new document and give it a name. Draw and arrange 3-4" lines with a 1 pt Stroke to display the Pattern Brushes for easy visual reference *(see layout on next page)*.

Go to any document where a Pattern Brush is applied to a path. Copy that path and paste it into the Pattern Brush document. Even if the path is only a straight line, all of its tiles, including corner and side tiles, will automatically load into the Brushes Panel. Apply the Pattern Brush to one of the lines in the Pattern Brush Document then delete the imported copy.

Repeat to **reuse** a saved Pattern Brush. Click on the path it's applied to in the Pattern Brush Document and paste the path into a new document.

The advantage to using this method is new Pattern Brushes can be added to the document at any time. To organize a large number of Pattern Brushes, consider saving multiple Pattern Brush documents based on type, i.e., floral, black and white, doodle art, linear, etc.

TIP: If individual Pattern Brush tiles need to be edited, click on the brush in the Brushes Panel, drag it onto the artboard, ungroup the tiles and edit. To add an edited tile back in, hold down the Option key and drag the tile back into the Brushes Panel in its proper tile location.

Sample Pattern Brush Document

Unlike a Pattern Brush Library, a dedicated Pattern Brush document can be added to at any time. It is great way to store and view favorite Pattern Brushes for future use. **To place a saved brush into a new document, select and copy a Pattern Brush path, then paste it into a new document.** All tiles, including corner tiles will be imported into that document's Brushes Panel.

What To Do If...

The Pattern Brush has thin white lines in between the pattern repeats.
The Bounding Box is probably not placed exactly around the design. Precision is important. View the tile in Outline Mode *(Command+Y)*. Zoom in close to identify where the problem is. If that doesn't work, delete the Bounding Box and create another one while in the Outline Mode. Remember to send it to the Back.

There is a line around the Pattern Brush.
The line is usually caused because there is a Stroke applied to the Bounding Box. Remove the Stroke and drag the tile back into the Brushes Panel.

Corner Tiles or End Tiles don't line up with the Side Tile.
Illustrator puts the Tiles where the Bounding Box tells it to, so the first thing to check is the Bounding Box. The Bounding Boxes for ALL the tiles in the Pattern Brush must be the same height. Place the tiles next to the Side Tile. If the Bounding Boxes are the same height, check to make sure the designs are placed correctly inside them so they align properly with the Side Tile. View in Outline Mode to locate where the problem is.

Corner Tiles are disfigured on the path.
When Corner Tiles get disfigured, it is either because the path isn't big enough or the angle is too small. Lower the weight of the path's Stroke in the Properties Panel or adjust the angle.

Corner Tile won't fit.
1) Make sure the Bounding Box has been sent to the back of the tile layer and try again.
2) If that doesn't work, start over. Go to Outline Mode to rotate the Side Tile, making sure the corners are exactly matched where they intersect. Draw a Bounding Box while in Outline Mode. Toggle in and out of that viewing mode to draw the design.
3) If that doesn't work, select an Auto Generated Option in the Pattern Brush Options Dialogue Box. Then go to the Brushes Panel and drag the Pattern Brush onto the artboard. Ungroup the tiles and compare the tile that isn't working to Illustrator's Auto Generated Corner Tile to determine what needs to be changed.

Error message says artwork contains an element that can't be used in a Pattern Brush.
At the time of the printing of this book, gradients and some swatches cannot be used in artwork for a Pattern Brush unless they are first Rasterized (*go to Object>Rasterize*). In older versions, artwork created in the "Draw Inside" mode must also be rasterized. Objects that are Rasterized are no longer vectors and can lose quality when enlarged. **EXCEPTION**: If artwork is being rejected because it contains text, convert the text to outlines. Select the text and go to Type>Create Outlines. The text will still be a vector but is no longer editable as text.

Problems encountered when trying to use a photograph as artwork for a Pattern Brush.
Photographs must be embedded before they can be placed as artwork in a Pattern Brush. The Embed button appears in the Quick Actions section of the Properties Panel when an unembedded photograph is selected. Illustrator may also require the photograph to be optimized if its resolution is too high to be used in a Pattern Brush. An error message pops up requesting approval to optimize the image. Click Ok. The photograph will be modified and added to the Brushes Panel.

There is no error message but Illustrator won't allow certain artwork to be drug into the Brushes Panel.
In some instances, a Tile has to be placed in the Swatches Panel first, and *then* selected from the drop-down tile menu in the Pattern Brush Options Dialogue Box. It still needs a Bounding Box. See Page 30 for instructions.

The Start and End Tiles are backwards.
If the wrong end of the Start and End Tiles attaches to the Pattern Brush Side Tile, they may be in the wrong location in the Brushes Panel. Swapping them should fix the problem.

The spacing is wrong between repeating tiles in a Pattern Brush.
Spacing is determined by the placement of the Pattern Brush and/or by Spacing Percentages added to the Pattern Brush Options Dialogue Box. Tweak the space added in the Bounding Box or change the percentage in the Spacing option until the desired spacing is achieved.

Corner tiles are too big in the Preview Panel of the Pattern Brush Options Dialogue Box.
This is not a problem. Corner tiles are not displayed to scale in the Preview Panel. They will always appear too big, even when they are the right size for the Pattern Brush. The only benefit to checking a corner tile in the Preview Panel is to make sure it is placed in the correct direction. Apply the Pattern Brush to a path to verify whether or not the corner is sized properly.

The Pattern Brush leaves gaps at the corners of a rectangle.
Corner tiles have not been assigned to the Pattern Brush or they are in the wrong position. In earlier versions of Illustrator, the tiles were arranged in a different order. Hover the cursor over a tile in the Pattern Brush Options Dialogue Box and the name of the tile will pop up.

The Pattern Brush is too large when applied to a Path.
To make a Pattern Brush smaller, change the Stroke weight of the path it is applied to in the Properties Panel. If it is still too large, resize the original design: go to Object>Transform>Scale. Check "Uniform" and enter a percentage below 100%. Scale Corners and Scale Strokes and Effects should be checked. If the resulting Stroke is too small, edit it in the Properties Panel. After the designs are resized, drag them into the Brushes Panel to create a new/smaller Pattern Brush.

Start and End Tiles of the Pattern Brush are distorted when applied to a curved path.
Pattern Brushes adopt a fluidity when applied to curved paths, and that includes all parts, even the Start and End Tiles. To use a brush where the ends will not be distorted on a curved path, **create an Art Brush instead of a Pattern Brush**. In the Art Brush Options Dialogue Box, the part that repeats and stretches can be specified while the rest of the brush stays in proportion. Art Brushes are created in one piece without tiles. They are also created horizontally. Drag the design into the Brushes Panel and when the New Brush Dialogue Box pops up, click on Art Brush. When the Art Brush Options Dialogue Box opens, click on Stretch Between Guides. Drag the guides to indicate which part of the brush is to stretch.

Creating Pattern Brushes is addictive and nothing else is getting done.
Call for carry-out.

Made in the USA
Monee, IL
05 November 2026

67387959R00038